EMPOWERING RURAL WOMEN

EMPOWERING RURAL WOMEN

(Through Dairy Cooperatives)

V.M. RAO

ANMOL PUBLICATIONS PVT. LTD.
NEW DELHI - 110 002 (INDIA)

ANMOL PUBLICATIONS PVT. LTD.
4374/4B, Ansari Road, Daryaganj
New Delhi - 110 002
Ph.: 23261597, 23278000
Visit us at: www.anmolpublications.com

Empowering Rural Women

First Published 2004
ISBN 81-261-1751-6

PRINTED IN INDIA

Published by J.L. Kumar for Anmol Publications Pvt. Ltd., New Delhi - 110 002 and Printed at Mehra Offset Press, Delhi.

Contents

Contents

Acknowledgements

The present book embodies the outcome of the report of a research project sponsored by Indian Council of Social Science Research, New Delhi. I owe a deep sense of gratitude to the ICSSR for their support and cooperation.

I would like to thank Dr. B.B. Barik, Director of the Institute for the encouragement and providing administrative support in conducting the study.

The present acknowledgements would be incomplete if did not thank the Managing Directors of APDDCF and KMF, Directors (STEP) of both the states, and General Managers of the selected milk unions. I have received help and cooperation from them in carrying out the study. The management of KMF deserve special thanks.

I am grateful to participants of 'National seminar on women dairy cooperatives', held at VMNICM during July 24-27, 2001 for their valuable suggestions on the recommendations included in this study. Thanks are also due to Mr. P. Sharma, my colleague at the Institute, for providing literature on self-help groups. During the process of data collection, I received help from a number of officials and non-officials whose names are also acknowledged in the end of the report. I sincerely acknowledge the help received from committee members, and employees of the selected WDCSs for providing minute details about functioning of the societies and village dynamics. They also helped in arranging meetings with women members.

Many thanks are due to sample respondents who cheerfully spared their time and parted with sensitive information sought from them. They gave free and frank opinions about their socio-economic status, and other relevant information. I was treated as member of their families. None of them, however, is responsible for the facts stated and opinions expressed in the report.

I am thankful to Miss. V. Srividya Rao who took pains in going through the draft and making necessary corrections.

Mr. V.U. Alone patiently typed the manuscript through its various versions and Miss. V. Yagneswari, and Miss. Pushpa Nadar helped in improving getup of the report.

—V. M. RAO

Chapter 1
Introduction

Introduction

Women represent half the world's human resources. Though women perform different roles [reproduction (only women), household (housework, food preparation, child earning,...), and productive (income generating activities)], women continue to be mainly responsible for 'care economy'. It is said that unpaid work of these women comes to around US $ 11 trillion/annum which is equivalent to half the world's GDP. But these income statistics are not entering national accounts, thus they are considered as invisible workers. But, women have excellent qualities like sacrificing, time consciousness, aesthetic and civic senses, willingness to take responsibilities, habit of thrift, and savings, and good managerial abilities.

The gender equality doctrine is an outstanding contribution of 20th century. The UN Declaration of Women's Rights (1967) postulated the egalitarian doctrine of achieving equal rights for women as that of men and advocated its universal necessity (Tapan, 2000). However, the ground realities are different. With 54% of working age women in the labour force as compared to over 80% male participation, the world is not making the most of its female talent and potentials (ILO, 2000). Further, women constitute 70% of world's 1.3 billion absolute poor. Approximately 20% of households worldwide are female-headed and this figure is increasing. In rural areas of Africa and Caribbean the proportion is more. Gender inequality persists in access to and control over productive resources, and in training, and retraining opportunities. Social norms severely restrict women's economic options by discouraging them from taking up jobs, limiting the range of tasks they may perform, defining child care as their duty, restricting their mobility, and promoting certain job option. In no country, women are treated on par with men, they are seen as second - rate citizens. According to Boserup (1970), 'to integrate women in the development process' is of vital importance for the chances of economic success. Not only does the overall development effort suffer if the potentials of the female labour force are neglected but women, children, and family like a whole are subjected to unnecessary strain and stress.... Since the productive use of human resources (male and female) is the key factor in development, much more attention should be given to the role women play-and the role could be playing-in development.' She also pointed out that women do not profit from 'modernization' in this same way as men. Other have defined such processes as the marginalization of women.

Indian Rural Women

The situation in India is not different from the world's scenario. Women had a high status in our society in good olden days. But in the process of evolution of so called development, the balance between men and women was disturbed (for more details see Department of Social Welfare, 1975). The society made them dependent; certain social restrictions were imposed on their lives so as to keep supremacy of men over women. Women are partly responsible for this sorry state of affairs. She herself respect a male child, provides hot food, hot water, good schooling, good clothes, providing meal first, special treatment... and this special treatment starts from day one. Because it is believed that son is "vamshodharak", "opens the doors of heaven" at the time of death, and insurance against risk in old age. There is a need to change the attitude and mind set of both men and women. There is need to make her self-reliant, bring awareness as to know her potential (a sleeping giant), equip her with necessary knowledge so as to participate in the decision in the decision making process/development process.

In a patriarchal society like ours, sons are greeted as joyous and economically beneficial additions to a household. At the same time, daughters are seen as financial drain since they wound up belonging to someone else's clan after marriage. Infanticide and ill treatment of baby girls were all too common. As a result, the female-male ratio in India has been going down, not only since independence but from the beginning of the present century (sex ratio has increased from 927 to 933 during 1991-2001 (Kundu, 2001). Further, women, as young girls, are constantly reminded of having a servile and submissive attitude since their childhood. Some of the disciplinary jargon includes being accommodative, adjusting and being able to compromise whenever there seems to be an inflammation of male ego. It is women who are expected to take on heavy burden of running home, hauling water far from long distances, carrying loads of firewood, and washing heavy clothes. One lesson women imbibe from their childhood is that they do not matter and their participation is practically non-existent at decision making levels. Similarly, in no society today do women enjoy equal opportunities as men. It is mainly due to : (a) low level of participation, (b) social, economic, cultural, and political restrictions, (c) inadequate/low access to and control over resources, (d) lack of training, and education, and (e) gender blind policies (ILO, 1995). Government of India has been taking initiatives, from time to time, to improve status of women.

Government Interventions

Constitution of India provided for equal rights and privileges for women and men. Directive principles of state policy embody the major policy goals of the welfare state. Article 39 (a) directs the state to frame its policy for ensuring that the citizens, men and women, equally have the right to have an adequate means of livelihood. Article 39 (d) directs the state to ensure equal pay for equal work for both men and women. Further, Central Social Welfare Board was established in 1953 to promote and assist NGOs in the field of women welfare, child development, and welfare of handicapped. Under community development programme, mahila mandals were promoted and supported since 1954.

A committee on status of women was constituted in 1975 which observed growing deterioration in the status of women (Department of Social Welfare, 1975). Subsequently, 1975-85 was declared as women's decade. Development of Women and Children in Rural Areas (DWACRA) was started as a sub-project of Integrated Rural Development Program (IRDP) on September 1, 1982 provide employment opportunities to women of rural families living below poverty line. National commission on self employed women and women in informal sector was constituted in 1988 which too indicated 'lack of access to credit, better technologies, and productive assets to women'. A separate chapter on women development was included in 6th Five Year Plan document. Eight Five Year Plan laid stress on empowerment of women. National Commission for Women was set up during 1992 to participate and advise on the planning process of socio-economic development of women (Planning Commission, 1993). Women studies centres were started in various universities to conduct research related to women development. Building up strengthening grass roots level women's organisations and groups, promoting participation of women in grass roots level democratic institutions were envisaged through 72nd and 73rd constitutional amendments (Batra, 1996). Very recently, the government has come up with proposal to set up National Resource Centre for Women for collecting and disseminating information, coordinating policy and programme related research and act as a focal point for all data and information relating to women' (Neelima, 2001). A bill is also pending with parliament to provide 1/3rd seats to women in both the houses. And finally Government of India has declared 2001 as Women's Empowerment year to acknowledge that one of the keys to our nation's socio-economic progress is empowerment of women and to create mass awareness of the linkages between development and women's empowerment on the one hand, and progress and gender equality on the other (Vajpayee, 2001).

The above initiatives tried by the Government of India for the upliftment of women can be summarised under five approaches: (a) welfare, (b) equity, (c) anti-poverty, (d) efficiency, and (e) empowerment. The welfare approach is one that benefits most vulnerable groups as possible recipients and is suitable at the initial stage of development. The equity approach takes special care of gender needs and emphasizes redistributing power. The anti-poverty approach recognises that a majority of women fall in the category of deprivation. It focusses on productive role of women. The efficiency approach takes care of practical gender needs and helps in improving capability and capacity of women by imparting education, skill, training, etc. The empowerment approach helps women in making their own choices with regard to their lives and makes them more active players in society. Thus, it is superior than the earlier approaches.

Women in Dairying

Dairy farming is a wide spread economic activity in India, transcending geographic and economic borders and women are recently beginning to be viewed as important contributors to milk production system. They are closely involved in tending, cleaning animals and sheds, cutting fodder, fetching grass, preparation of dung cakes, reproduction, milking, preparation of milk products, marketing, and representation in organisation of cooperatives.

It is estimated that women contribute as much as 75-85% of total labour requirement of dairy farming (Rao, 1996; Rao, 1997; and Rao 2000). Due to the efforts taken by the NDDB and other state level dairy federations, women are encouraged to participate actively in planning and management of primary dairy cooperatives. Women form around 20-22% of total dairy cooperative membership. Further, there are as many as 3000 all women dairy cooperative societies (WDCSs) working in the country (Chennegowda, 2000). Main aim of promoting WDCSs is to provide employment, income, and increased status for rural women, and thus aim at overall development of women.

Indo-Swiss-Andhra Pradesh Women Extension Project

It was launched in Visakhapatnam, Vizianagaram, West Godavari, Krishna, Khammam, Mahaboobnagar, and Cuddapah districts of Andhra Pradesh in 1976. Major objective of the program was to cooperate in the field of cattle breeding, fodder production, and dairy development. Specific objectives were to: (a) encourage women to participate in the development of dairying and animal husbandry, (b) develop women specific activities, and (c) establish and reinforce a women oriented extension service. The programme succeeded in setting up of an extension framework to facilitate involvement of rural women in informal groups. It organised number of WDCSs, and milk collection centers by women. Certain awareness and knowledge on modern techniques of cattle breeding was created (Ramaswamy and Kesavan, 1994).

Ford Foundation Project on Women Empowerment

Ford foundation launched a pilot project in 1983 to integrate rural women into dairy cooperative societies in Chittoor, Krishna, and Nalgonda districts of Andhra Pradesh. Major objective of the programme was to motivate, organise, and enroll women as members of WDCSs. Specific objectives of the programme were: (a) to organise WDCSs , (b) to persuade male members to transfer their membership to women, (c) to train women producers in modern methods of dairying, (d) to provide credit to poor women for purchase of milch animals, (e) to provide revolving funds to WDCSs to secure bank loans for members, (f) to train rural women in management of dairy cooperatives inparting skills. To achieve this objective, the programme promoted a network of women extension supervisors to implement women extension work under the guidance of a programme coordinator. As many as 400 WDCSs were organised and the initial response was good. A national seminar on women dairy cooperatives was held at Tirupathi to review progress made during December 20-22, 1985.

However, the programme failed to achieve the objectives due to poor cooperative development, insufficient education, and extension and lack of commitment from APDDCF (Anonymous, 1988, Anonymous, 1989, and Ramaswamy and Kesavan, 1994).

Integrating Women into Mainstream Dairying

The project aims at promoting all women dairy cooperative societies and sought to create opportunities of asset formation and income generation for women drawn from economically and socially backward communities. The programme was aided by the Government of The Netherlands during 1987-94 and was implemented in Prakasam district of Andhra Pradesh. Specific objectives of the programme were (a) to generate active participation of women in village economy, (b) to ensure that women learn to cooperate in their economic ventures, (c) to bring about a economic equality and social justice by focusing attention on and directing training towards poor women, and (d) to empower women to be able to move into positions of decision making and power within their society. As many as 77 women groups and 55 WDCSs were registered with a total membership of 6426. The programme went on well during the initial years and failed soon after withdrawal of Government support. There was hardly any component of training in this programme. For more details on the project, see Madhavan, et al. (1992), and Ramaswamy and Kesavan (1994).

NDDB's Efforts in Empowering Women

National Dairy Development Board through its cooperative development (CD) programme (1986-96) promoted the empowerment of women dairy farmers as one dimension of a large efforts to strengthen dairy cooperatives. The CD team contained five trained officers to conduct a member education programme for women in villages through group discussions, question and answer sessions, and group singing. The women instructors conveyed empowering ideas to women dairy farmers in a three day training programme in each village.

A major aspect of the CD programme was to empower women by brining them into decision making process of their cooperative (Wayangankar and Singh, 1992). According to Sharma and Vanjani (1989) CD programme means obtaining employment, income, and improved status for women farmers in their rural environment. By participating in various activities organised through CD programme, women dairy farmers engaged themselves in a variety of developmental and self-employed activities (Rogers, Singhal, Wayangankar, and Shefner, 1993). Rogers and Singhal (1993) were of the opinion that women acting in solidarity had power that cannot be achieved by one women alone.

STEP Programme

Support to training and employment programme for women (STEP) was launched in 1986 as a measure to ensure well being of women in traditional informal sectors. It was sponsored by the Department of Women and Child Development, Ministry of Human Resource Development, Government of India (for more details on STEP, see appendix 1.1). It aims at increasing self reliance and autonomy of women by enhancing their productivity and enabling them to take up income generation activities (animal husbandry, dairying, poultry, sericulture, fisheries, etc.). A number of state level dairy federations (Andhra Pradesh, Bihar, Madhya Pradesh, Maharashtra, Orissa, Karnataka, Rajasthan, Uttaranchal, Uttar Pradesh, West Bengal, etc.) took up organising WDCSs under STEP programme. Government of India provides, on an average, Rs. 1.50 lakh/WDCS and half of it is towards training and sensitization. Training programmes for secretaries, testers, management committee members, and chairpersons on dairy animal management, artificial insemination, gender sensitization, health and nutrition, legal literacy, weaning foods, etc. are being proposed. It is expected that such awareness coupled with income generation activity would empower women.

Empowerment

Any attempt to improve their status should start with empowerment. It is the process through which individuals gain efficacy, defined as the degree to which an individual perceives that he or she controls his or her environment (Bandura, 1986). According to Hapke (1992), empowerment should include (a) access to and control over productive resources, (b) knowledge and awareness of ones self and society, and of personal needs, health issues, legal rights, technological innovations, and availability of social and economic resources and how to take advantage of them, (c) self image, and (d) autonomy. Female empowerment approach stresses the capacity of women to increase their self-reliance and internal strength. It aims at restructuring of gender relations within both family and in society at large, and it is society's recognition of women's equality with men. Further, it is an accepted fact that fruits of development are most equitably distributed and enjoyed equitably when development strategies are women centered.

According to Srilatha (1994), empowerment is a process of challenging existing power relations, and of gaining greater control over sources of power. Karl (1995) opines that empowerment of women involves four interrelated and mutually reinforcing components: collective awareness and capacity building and skills development; participation and greater control; decision making power; and action to bring about gender equality. Thus, it implies control over decision making process, both at personal and cooperative, control over income and expenditure, and acquisition and exercise of knowledge. It has four dimensions: economic, social, political, and psychological. Empowerment of people requires action on: (a) investing in education and health of the people so that they can take advantage of market opportunities, (b) ensuring an enabling environment that gives everyone access to credit and productive assets so that playing fields of lives are more even, and (c) empowering both women and men so that they can compete on equal footing. It gives people of a community the ability and opportunity to take part in decision making process with regard to socio-economic and political issues affecting their existence. Empowerment of the deprived begins with their ability to voice their opinion through the process of consensuses politics and dialogue, backed up by access to education, information, organisation, employment, and credit (Sengupta, 1998).

Despite various theoretical approaches to the concept of empowerment, we hardly find any study except Rao, et al. (1995). 12 variables are identified to measure empowerment. Some of them are specific to empowerment of women dairy farmers, while others are general to women. They are coded as '3' if the women alone attended it, responses are coded as '2' if such decision involved her husband too, and '1' if her husband alone involved. Thus, total empowerment score could range from 12 to 36.

Objectives

The overall objective of this study is to understand the nature and impact of STEP programme on women and to draw lessons for future policy exercises. The specific objectives of the study are:

(1) to study performance of 'all women dairy cooperative societies' (WDCSs) in different agro-climatic regions;

(2) to calculate quantitative and qualitative changes in women covered under STEP programme;

(3) to observe the differential decision making pattern of farm women in various animal husbandry tasks;

(4) to develop an empowerment scale for women dairy farmers; and

(5) to document working of self-help groups among respondents.

Methodology

The study was conducted in two major south Indian states: Andhra Pradesh, and Karnataka . Based on the agro-climatic conditions, livestock intensity, and development of cooperative dairying three milk unions/state were selected. A list of WDCSs having the age of three years and more was obtained from the selected milk unions, and arranged in descending order on the basis of annual milk procurement separately for STEP and NON-STEP WDCSs. From each category (STEP and NON-STEP), four WDCSs are selected randomly. Care was taken to select societies with similar age, membership, procurement, etc. so as to make appropriate comparisons. Finally, five women members/WDCS are interviewed with the help of a pre-tested questionnaire. Data on livestock holding, involvement in WDCS activities, participation in decision making, social status, nutrition, health care, time allocation, attitude towards girl child, etc. were collected during April 2000—February 2001.

Thus, 240 members from 48 WDCSs spread over six districts (Prakasam, Warangal, and Chittoor from Andhra Pradesh, and Bangalore, Belgaum, and Bellary-Raichur from Karnataka) constituted the sampling frame. List of selected WDCSs is provided in appendix 1.2 and their approximate location is given in maps 1.1 and 1.2 respectively for Andhra Pradesh and Karnataka. Secondary data on performance (membership, procurement, sales, products manufactured, input services provided, net profits, etc.) of unions, and selected WDCSs, composition of management committee members, organisation of meetings, etc. are also collected. Extensive discussions are held with a number of officials during visits and a list of officials contacted is given in appendix 1.3.

Data Processing

All the data collected are feed to computer and necessary charts/graphs/tables, means, standard deviations, etc. are prepared using SPSS package.

Map 1.1: Approximate Location of Selected WDCSs in Andhra Pradesh

Map 1.2: Approximate Location of Selected WDCSs in Karnataka

Organisation of the Report

The report is organised in 10 chapters. Chapter 1 gives introduction to the study. It deals with status of women, government interventions, women in dairying, few programmes aimed at involving women in dairying, objectives, and methodology. Chapter 2 is devoted to review the progress of APDDCF and selected milk unions thereof, while chapter 3 looked at KMF and the selected unions. Performance of STEP and NON-STEP WDCSs is evaluated in chapter 4, and case studies of selected WDCSs are provided in chapter 5. Chapter 6 deals with an overview of selected respondents under three subheadings: (a) socio-economic status of respondents, (b) decision making pattern of women, and (c) impact of STEP on women. Empowerment scales comprised the content of chapter 7, and brief account of women's involvement in self-help groups is discussed in chapter 8. Chapter 9 contains profiles of selected respondents, and finally chapter 10 included summary, and recommendations.

REFERENCES

1. Biswas (1999) developed 11 indicators of women's empowerment. They included (1) mobility, (2) decision making power, (3) autonomy, (4) economic security, (5) freedom from domination by the family, (6) political and legal awareness, (7) participation in public protests and political campaign, (8) contribution to family expenditure or income, (9) reproductive right, (10) exposure to information, and (11) participation in development programmes. Empowerment index was developed in three stages: empowerment index for individual items of an indicator was formulated, empowerment index of an indicator consisting of different issues under each indicator was constructed, and finally the overall empowerment index consisting of different indicators was developed. It was purely a theoretical exercise with no quantification.

2. In general, performance of Karnataka Cooperative Milk Producers' Federation (KMF) is better than Andhra Pradesh Dairy Development Cooperative Federation (APDDCF). There is a separate department of STEP having 10 officials and headed by a Director at KMF while it is looked after by a programme officer with skeleton staff/resources at APDDCF. The data and reports are upto date and readily available at KMF while it is dismal at APDDCF.

Chapter 2

Profiles of APDDCF and Selected Unions

Background

An attempt is made in this chapter to provide an overview of APDDCF, and selected milk union (Prakasam, Chittoor and Warangal). Performancel is measured in terms of membership procurement, sale of fluid milk, other milk products, turnover, net profit/net loss, etc.

Andhra Pradesh is a large state in southern India and lies entirely within tropics. It has a geographical area of 2.77 lakh sq. kms. and is bounded on north-east by Orissa; north and north-west by Madhya Pradesh, and Maharashtra; Karnataka in west; Tamil Nadu in south; and Bay of Bengal in east. About 24% of the area is under forests. There is intensive irrigation and farming in deltas of Krishna and Godavari rivers. Rice is the main food crop, but maize, millet, and pulses are also grown. Cash crops like tobacco, cotton, chillies, oilseeds, and sugarcane are cultivated.

Dairy Development in Andhra Pradesh

Dairy industry travelled a long way from yester years when dairying and milk supply schemes in the state were implemented by Milk Commissioner, Director of Animal Husbandry, and Registrar of Cooperative Societies. Dairying, of late, in the state has assumed new dimensions as a strategy for rural development and for eradicating poverty, and under-employment of small, marginal farmers and agricultural labourers. Milk production constituted 11% of the state's agricultural economy (1995). The state has one of the largest bovine population in the country. District-wise bovine population and milk production are provided in Table 2.1. Chittoor district has highest crossbreeds while Mahboobnagar has local cows. Milk production is the highest in Guntur followed by Chittoor, and Krishna.

Table 2.1

Districtwise Breedable Bovine Population (Lakhs) and Milk Production in Andhra Pradesh, 1993-94

District	*Crossbreds*	*Local cows*	*Buffaloes*	*Milk production (tonnes)*
Adilabad	0.5	173.9	83.8	NA
Anantapur	6.1	144.9	154.3	119
Chittoor	125.9	141.9	89.6	297
Cuddapah	2.9	33.9	229.9	119
East Godavari	8.8	83.6	254.7	247
Guntur	1.2	22.9	401.5	315
Hyderabad	0.6	0.8	9.2	16
Karimnagar	3.4	90.9	176.0	189
Khammam	0.3	171.1	225.4	NA
Krishna	3.4	34.3	360.6	268
Kurnool	1.0	107.9	226.5	144
Mahboobnagar	4.6	199.9	159.7	139
Medak	1.4	87.1	133.0	127
Nalgonda	2.8	146.6	258.6	161
Nellore	0.8	70.8	294.2	196
Nizamabad	1.1	62.6	122.9	94

(Contd.)

District	*Crossbreds*	*Local cows*	*Buffaloes*	*Milk production (tonnes)*
Prakasam	0.8	36.2	384.6	240
Ranga Reddy	4.6	65.2	109.0	140
Srikakulam	14.1	160.8	55.8	76
Visakhapatnam	6.1	69.7	186.1	138
Vizianagaram	6.2	102.5	102.6	95
Warangal	1.4	105.7	173.9	110
West Godavari	5.4	60.0	255.6	299
Total	203.3	2173.5	4445.0	3766

Source: Records of APDDCF.

Planning for dairy development in Andhra Pradesh was started with introduction of a Pilot Milk Supply Scheme at Hyderabad in 1960. This has turned into a gigantic Integrated Milk Project with assistance of UNICEF. It donated equipment for dairy at Hyderabad and Milk Products Factory (MPF) at Vijayawada. Till then there was no organised procurement and sale of milk in the state. Recognising economic benefits of dairying and vast scope for employment opportunities for rural people state government has invested Rs. 818 lakhs till the end of Fourth Five Year Plan for dairy development. Efforts were made to establish Andhra Pradesh dairy development department in 1971.

Genesis and Growth of Andhra Pradesh Dairy Development Corporation (APDDC)

The APDDC was constituted (1974) for application of commercial principles in working of dairy industry and to preserve cost consciousness and proper resource utilisation. Subsequently, all dairy units including feed mixing plants under the control of government departments were transferred to administrative control of the corporation. Later, Operation Flood Programme-I (OFP) was implemented in Guntur district in 1977. It has created a tremendous impact on milk producers in providing technical inputs within their reach by district union besides regular payment and bonus to producers. With success of OFP-I in Guntur, Government has accepted to implement OFP-II in 16 districts of Andhra Pradesh. During this period, APDDC was converted into Andhra Pradesh Dairy Development Cooperative Federation Limited (APDDCF) which began functioning from November, 1981. Main objectives of the federation are (a) to provide assured year-round market for surplus milk produced in rural areas, (b) to supply wholesome milk and milk products to urban consumers, and (c) to stimulate milk production and to develop required infrastructure. Its mission is professionalisation and decentralisation of management of dairy cooperatives to function with profitability with thrust on industrialisation of rural dairying. Organisation of primary Dairy Cooperative Societies (DCS) on Anand pattern, organising training programmes and visits of milk producers to Anand, and exposure to functioning of dairy cooperatives have motivated and created great awareness and confidence among milk producers to manage their own organisations. During Operation Flood-III, Nellore district and expansion of dairies at Visakha, and Rajahmundry were taken up. Further, few chilling centres were also covered during this period. Surplus milk is converted into various milk products like WMP, SMP, bay food, ghee, pasteurised table butter, cheese and marketed throughout the country under the brand name of 'Vijaya'. Besides frozen products like ice-cream, kulfi, chacobar, flavoured milk, and milk shake are also being marketed through various dairy parlours.

The federation implemented Integrated Dairy Development Project with financial assistance from NCDC and Government of Andhra Pradesh, covering non-operation flood districts of Khammam, Warangal, and Karimnagar with a total outlay of Rs. 17.50 crores. Technology mission for dairy development has been taken up in 16 districts of the state to consolidate development achieved so far in association with different departments (animal husbandry, DRDA, SC/BC corporation, commercial banks, etc.) to enhance milk production and consumption.

Table 2.2

Growth in Selected Indicators of APDCF, 1991-00

Year	*DC*	*Milk suppliers (laksh)*	*Milk chilling centre*	*Avg. procure- ment//day (lakhs litres)*	*Avg. sales/day lakh*	*Capacity utilisa- tion (%)*	*No. of emplo- yees*
1990-91	4397	5.03	61	7.91	5.57	48	8512
1991-92	4959	6.05	62	8.49	6.05	52	8863
1992-93	5283	7.58	63	9.70	6.68	54	8836
1993-94	5005	6.86	63	9.55	6.38	53	8784
1994-95	4703	6.19	63	7.55	6.36	47	8792
1995-96	4495	5.23	58	6.29	6.36	33	8753
1996-97	4332	5.70	59	6.81	5.93	35	7947
1997-98	4275	5.93	61	8.53	6.21	43	7297
1998-99	4270	5.67	65	8.95	6.62	44	7132
1999-00							

Source: Records of APDDCF.

There are 4270 DCSs (equal number of producers associations) with over 5.67 lakh milk suppliers (Table 2.2). However, capacity utilisation against installed capacity is only 44% and varied across unions. In all, there are about 7000 employees working in various unions in addition to equal number of employees working at DCSs. Further, over 400 'all women dairy cooperative societies' (WDCSs) are also organised under various developmental projects and about 15% of the total members are women (Table 2.3). Of the total members, 20% are landless labourers, 30% marginal, 32% small, and 18% 'others'.

Table 2.3

Distribution of Dairy Cooperatives in Andhra Pradesh

Name of the Milk Sheds	*Village dairy cooperatives*				*Farmer members*		*Avg. milk Procurement (litres/day)*
	Organised		*Functional*				
	Anand pattern	*Others*	*Anand pattern*	*Others*	*Total*	*Women*	
Chittoor	889	526	887	526	66250	13418	179.86
Cuddapah	294	241	284	241	25698	5488	27.32
Godavari	538	234	459	234	59005	4699	11.30
Guntur	634	136	618	136	126067	22060	122.99
Krishna	447	360	409	360	66046	8329	78.38
Kurnool	275	---	234	---	34800	5680	20.63
Nalgonda	395	329	301	329	33817	4985	31.86
Nellore	280	377	256	328	31671	5304	29.45
Nizamabad	348	---	329	---	35578	2368	20.18
Prakasam	382	410	372	378	64090	12818	73.80
Visaka	651	478	631	478	97370	15442	140.59
Total	5133	3091	4780	3010	640392	100591	736.36

Source: NDDB quarterly report 1998.

Vision 2020

Government of Andhra Pradesh has prepared a vision document 2020 (perspective plan) and envisaged goals for 2010. It has rightly identified dairying as an important growth-engine. Accordingly, the document envisaged that DCSs would increase from 4548 in 1998-99 to 17241 by 2009-10 and that of membership from 7.40 lakhs to 23.32 lakhs during the same period. As of women membership, the vision document projected that it would reach 11.86 lakhs by 2009-10 (Table 2.4). It is hoped that milk production would increase by 7% annum, and per capital availability milk from 174 ml in 1998-99 to 230 ml by 2009-10.

Table 2.4

Targets Included in Vision 2020 Document

Sl. No.	*Particulars*	*1998-99*	*2009-10*
1.	DCSs organised	4548	17241
2.	Membership (lakhs)	7.40	23.32
3.	Women members (lakhs)	1.29	11.86
4.	Milk production (lakh litres/day)	118.63	245.60
5.	Procurement (lakh litres/day)	9.11	70.95
6.	Milk sales (lakh litres/day)	6.51	34.32

Source: Records of APDDCF.

Dairy Programmes for Rural Women

Organisation of WDCSs have been taken up, to enhance status of women by inducting them into dairying, with financial assistance from Ford Foundation, Government of The Netherlands, and Indo-Swiss project (for details, please refer Chapter 1). These societies are being managed by the women themselves. Of late, WDCSs are being organised under Support to Training and Employment Programme for Women (STEP), Department of Women and Child Development, Ministry of Human Resources Development, Government of India. The Government sanctioned Rs. 11.54 crores for organising WDCSs in 20 districts (8 from coastal region, 3 from Rayalaseema, and 9 from Telangana). The project envisaged organisation of a 580 WDCSs with 26000 women membership. Milk unions/milk shades were conceived as nodal agencies for implementation for the program. Voluntary organisations, departments of a women and chill welfare, DRDAs, SC/ST/BC corporations, departments of adult education, departments of medical and health, departments of animal husbandry, etc. were identified as sister organisations. By the end of 3rd year, the federation organised 339 WDCSs with a membership of 17165. As against the sanctioned amount of Rs. 11.54 crores the federation utilized Rs. 436.88 lakhs (38% utilization). Progress of WDCSs organised under STEP is provided in Table 2.5 and union/milkshed-wise distribution of WDCSs and membership is presented in Table 2.6 Chittoor has 60 WDCSs with 2707 membership. Prakasam, Chittoor, and Warangal milk unions are covered under this programme in the state which was started in 1997-98. An attempt is made in the following sections to provide a succinct review of selected milk unions of the state. Criteria for selection of districts was provided in methodology (Chapter 1).

Table 2.5

Progress of WDCSs Organised under STEP in Andhra Pradesh

Year	*WDCSs*	*Membership*
1st year	123	7599
2nd year	216	10016
3rd year	339	17615

Source: Records of the APDDCF.

Table 2.6

Union/milkshed-wise WDCSs Organised under STEP in Andhra Pradesh

Union/Milkshed	*WDCSs Organised*	*Membership*
Visakha	15	1128
Krishna	35	2754
Prakasam	45	1691
Nellore	25	1544
Chittoor	60	2707
Kurnool	20	957
Nalgonda-Ranga Reddy	25	1136
Karimnagar-Adilabad	15	496
Medak-Nizamabad	25	1431

(Contd.)

Union/Milkshed	*WDCSs Organised*	*Membership*
Warangal	32	1563
Khammam	10	492
Mahaboobnagar	20	1073
Total	339	17615

Source: Records of the APDDCF.

Prakasam District Milk Producers Cooperative Union Limited

Milk production in Prakasam district started with commissioning of a milk chilling centre at Ongole in 1975. Majority of milk producers in the district are landless agricultural labours, marginal and small farmers and it is one of the backward districts of Andhra Pradesh. The cotton calamity of 1986 in the district forced majority of medium/ small farmers to dairying as a dependable source of income. Hence, dairying is an important subsidiary income to farming and non-farming community of the district. This led to awareness about scientific milk production practices in the district. The milk producers' union as also the department of animal husbandry had contributed to this development.

Table 2.7

Milk Procurement Network at Prakasam

Unit	*No. of milk procurement*	*No. of Mandals*	*No. of milk collection*		
			DCSs	*MPACs*	*Total*
Ongole	14 (13 link routes)	32	274	57	331
Kanigiri	8 (1 link route)	6	18	130	148
Cumbum	2	3	5	35	40
Y. Palem	6 (1 link route)	6	31	112	143
K. Manjulur	5 (3 link routes)	9	98	21	119

Source: Records of the union.

Table 2.8

Growth in Selected Indicators of Prakasam Milk Union, 1991-00

Year	*DCSs*	*Milk suppliers (lakhs)*	*Average procure-ment/day*	*Average sales/day (lakh litres)*	*Capacity utiliza-tion (%)*	*Number of employ-ees*
1990-91	292	0.54	0.82	0.05	67	167
1991-92	348	0.72	0.83	0.08	68	288
1992-93	382	1.20	0.90	0.12	47	281
1993-94	412	0.74	0.91	0.10	48	264
1994-95	445	0.75	0.79	0.13	41	279
1995-96	368	0.76	0.69	0.14	23	300
1996-97	331	0.75	0.74	0.16	25	262
1997-98	361	0.53	0.82	0.17	27	223
1998-99	344	0.39	0.83	0.17	28	229
1999-00						

Source: Records of the union.

The Prakasam district cooperative milk producers' union limited was organised in 1986 with affiliation of DCSs formed on Anand pattern. By this time, the union has an installed capacity of 80000 litres/day. Investment (Rs. 19.25 crores) from OFP-II strengthened processing capacity up to 3.50 lakh litres/day besides introduction of milk production enhancement inputs at doorsteps of producers. The milk products factory has the capacity to handle 25000 litres milk sachets/day, 25 tonnes of butter/day, 10 tonnes of ghee/day, and 30 tonnes of powder/day. There are four milk chilling centres (Kondamanjulur, Kanigiri, Yeragondapalem, and Cumbum) with an installed capacity of 0.84 lakh litres/day. Apart from fluid milk of various grades, milk products like butter milk, white butter, pasteurised table butter, khova, and sterilised flavoured milk are manufactured at Ongole (main dairy). Milk procurement network and distribution of DCSs at the union are provided in Table 2.7. In all, there are 56 mandals (tehsils) and union covered all mandals. The union has 426 DCSs, and 355 Milk Producers Association Centres covering 1.06 lakh producer members. Of the total membership, 20% are women producers. Agricultural labours and marginal farmers constituted as much as 43% of the total membership followed by 49% from small and medium land holdings, and rest (8%) are large farmers. Caste-wise, 3% are STs, 11% are SCs, 21% are BCs, and 65% are 'others'.

Due to constant efforts of the union and involvement of producers, average milk procurement of 5000 litres/day in 1976 increased to an average of 95,000 litres/day in 1993-94. As against 426 registered DCSs, 344 (80%) are functional (Table 2.8). There is no trend in DCSs and milk suppliers. As a result of this, union average came down and started declining since 1997-98. Capacity utilisation of the union is one of the lowest in the state which needs special attention of the management. Half the DCSs (211) and the union were superceded in 1999 which is partly responsible for fall in various parameters considered in Table 2.8. Further, as a result of government's liberalisation policy, more than 20 private dairies had come up in the district. These dairies are eating into the profits/ procurement of the union. The union has facilities to manufacture butter milk, white butter, pasteurised table butter, cooking butter, khova, and sterilised flavoured milk.

Entire Prakasam district has been gripped by severe drought in 2000. Government initially declared 31 mandals as drought hit and later included all 56 mandals due to pressure from people. Mandals like Markapur, Giddalur, Kanigiri, Cumbum, and Yerragondapalem had witnessed acute drinking water scarcity and fodder shortages for five months. Prakasm, known for its internationally reputed 'Ongole bull' is today is not in a position to protect its cattle wealth due to water scarcity.

Under technical inputs programme, the union provides breeding bulls, promotes AI centres, undertakes animal health care activities, supply fodder seeds, cattle feed, electronic milko-testers, and training to farmers/employees.

Women Dairy Project

Government of India sanctioned a women dairy project (WDP) under STEP to organise 580 WDCSs with 25,760 women members during 1998-2000 in Andhra Pradesh. Prakasam took the responsibility of organising 60 women WDCSs with 2400 members.

Project Area

Markapur division is dominated by tribal population with rainfed agriculture as the main source of income for the people. Scanty rainfall, annual droughts, and lack of agricultural work are features of this area. As a result, most of labour, and small/marginal farmers migrate to neighbouring districts (Guntur, Krishna, Nellore, and Chittoor) for work for 4-5 months a year. Malnutrition is prevailing in the area and only 21% of the population are literate. Socio-economic survey was conducted in the command area of Yerragondapalem MCC and 15 villages were identified in the first year (1997-98). They are eight from Dornal mandal, four from Pullalacheruvu, and three from Yerragondapalem.

There are 793 members, out of which 545 are SCs, 8 STs, 131 BCs, and OCs are 109. Soon after organisation of 15 WDCSs, paid secretaries and testers (women) of these societies underwent training. On successful completion of training, milk collection was started from September, 1997. All the 15 centres were supplied with equipment like furniture, testing equipment, records, name boards, and fodder seeds. Further, de-wormicides, first-aid medicines, travis, foot and mouth vaccines, and HS vaccines were supplied to all the 15 WDCSs.

Good India, a non-governmental organisation was nominated to implement some components of WDP. Surveys were conducted in villages where there are thrift and DWCRA groups. While selecting members, preference was given to women headed families, widows, handicapped and migrating women. WDCSs are organised ranging from 40-60 members/WDCS. Election of office bearers to these societies was unanimous and educated women were selected for undergoing training to work as secretaries, milk testers, AI workers, etc. at Ongole dairy. Looking at the enthusiasm and sincerity shown by these women, 800 dairy animals under IRDP with 50% subsidy was sanctioned by the district administration. SC/ST/BC corporations sanctioned 20% margin money. Prakasam milk union gave 15% of the project cost as short term loan, and the balance 15% was borne by the women. All the animals were insured under master policy. Thus, the entire exercise was a collaboration among various organisations associated with rural development and deserves emulation. Though there was a moratorium of one year in repayment, majority of the producers, had started repayment soon after grounding the scheme, and 20% had already repaid the entire loan. Looking at the success, milk union provided a veterinary doctor and cattle feed to the tune of Rs. 2.00 lakhs under DPAP. Some of the members were taken on educational trips/tours too. Home science graduates were engaged for training women in preparation of weaning foods, nutritious diet, sanitation, etc. Further, 30 villages were surveyed and 12 identified for implementation of 2nd phase of the programme in Yerragondapalem; Pullalachervu, and Thripurantakam mandals in the district.

Organised Dairying in Chittoor District

Chittoor district occupies an important position in dairying map of Andhra Pradesh. Milk collection was started by organising milk supply unions at Chittoor/Srikalahasti/Puttur/Kanigiri during 1940-45. Actual participation of producers was started after intensive milk supply scheme (IMMS) (1969) and establishment of a dairy in Chittoor. Under IMMS, village level milk collection was organised with producers headed by their informally elected representative as group leader. Quality based pricing was practised under the supervision of dairy officials. In order to popularise dairying in the district, chilling centres at Pichatur, and Srikalahasti (eastern region), and Madanapalle, V. Kota, and Pileru (western region) were started (Table 2.9).

Table 2.9

Infrastructure of Milk Processing at Chittoor Milk Union

Sl. No.	Unit	Location	Year of starting	Initial handling capacity (lakhs) litres/day)	Handling capacity (2000)
1.	Chittoor	Chittoor	Dec '69	0.12	2.00
2.	MCC	Pichatur	Aug '77	0.06	0.22
3.	MCC	Madanapalle	Mar '79	0.12	0.50
4.	MCC	Srikalahasti	Mar '79	0.06	0.15
5.	MCC	V. Kota	Oct '80	0.06	0.27
6.	MCC	Piler	Feb '85	0.06	0.45

Source: Records of the union.

The district was included under OFP-II and an amount of Rs. 3.92 crores were spent during 1983-87. Subsequently, district milk union was registered in October, 1988. Milk products factory is located on 28 acres on the outskirts of Chittoor town. An amount of Rs. 2.53 crores was sanctioned for further expansion under OFP III. As regards composition of membership, 3% are STs, 14.3% are SCs, 25% are BCs, and 57.7% are 'others'. About 31% of the members are agricultural labourers, 22% marginal farmers, 29% small farmers, 11% medium, and 7% large farmers. Of the total membership, 23% are women.

Milk procurement started in 1969-70 (Table 2.10), and stood at 3.54 lakh litres was the collection during that year, and increased steadily. Installed capacities for various products at the main dairy are given Table 2.11 and growth in production of these products are presented in Table 2.12. Progress in health care facilities provided by the milk union is presented in Table 2.13.

Table 2.10
Unit-wise Progress in Procurement at Chittoor (lakh litres), 1970-00

Year	*Chittoor (Dec'67)*	*Puchatur (Aug'77)*	*Madanapalle (Mar'79)*	*Srikalasti*	*Piler (Feb'81)*	*V.Kota (Oct'80)*	*Total*
1969-70	3.54						3.54
1970-71	9.00						9.00
1971-72	5.16						15.16
1972-73	9.20						9.20
1973-74	14.11						14.11
1974-75	20.19						20.12
1975-76	38.79						38.79
1976-77	77.63	0.25					77.88
1977-78	109.17	5.09					114.26
1978-79	156.51	11.33	6.30				174.34
1979-80	146.33	11.42	12.85	3.20	73.00	0.00	246.80
1980-81	137.83	9.83	14.86	5.49	72.77	3.71	244.43
1981-82	170.78	12.40	20.74	6.02	15.08	5.14	230.16
1982-83	250.00	20.33	38.57	13.84	37.38	12.64	372.76
1983-84	245.90	18.50	55.71	11.80	43.68	11.77	387.36
1984-85	274.90	18.50	55.71	9.45	11.95	12.70	383.21
1985-86	337.50	25.25	62.59	13.84	38.48	14.29	491.95
1986-87	382.29	33.77	59.86	18.09	41.53	15.42	550.95
1987-88	395.71	35.19	54.55	18.19	41.97	16.56	562.17
1988-89	460.32	29.49	57.30	15.55	66.00	19.11	647.77
1989-90	506.06	32.17	80.57	12.31	92.32	25.26	748.69
1990-91	460.59	28.13	97.34	12.34	108.89	30.70	737.99
1991-92	412.32	21.13	101.71	12.81	89.62	37.47	675.06
1992-93	424.96	29.02	93.81	20.69	86.60	49.48	704.56
1993-94	320.83	23.36	77.67	16.68	65.79	77.31	555.52
1994-95	176.50	13.48	27.59	6.94	35.48	19.34	279.26
1995-96	164.50	14.46	10.87	5.74	13.69	12.39	221.28
1996-97	164.47	13.72	19.09	6.87	12.46	19.15	234.78
1997-98	151.28	16.36	33.90	10.71	18.83	17.78	248.90
1998-99	188.22	21.50	39.95	13.82	22.21	12.98	298.33
1999-00	175.00	10.90	32.34	10.92	18.89	11.11	259.15

Source: Records of the union.

Table 2.11
Milk Products Factory, Chittoor

Product	*Processing (tonnes/day)*	*Storage*	*Packing*
Cheddar cheese	2.70 (3 shifts)	150 MT cold store	---
Processed cheese	3.30 (3 shifts)	---	3.3 tonnes/day (3 shifts)
Butter	12.00 (3 shifts)	Deep freeze 200 MT	---
Ghee	8.00 (3 shifts)	9.00 tonnes bulk in tanks	15 kg. 1 kg, ½ kg and 200 grams (3 shifts/day)
Fluid milk		1.05 lakh litres	2.30 lakh litres/day

Source: Records of the union.

Table 2.12
Growth in Production of Milk Products (tonnes)

Year	*SMP*	*WMP*	*Ghee*	*Processed cheese*	*Butter*
1982-83	1705	108	1029	156	291
1983-84	1854	43	974	210	297
1984-85	1718	835	1304	144	157
1985-86	1742	488	1501	197	00
1986-87	1085	195	1061	129	17
1987-88	2560	1379	2383	262	165
1988-89	2361	5560	1742	242	927
1989-90	2369	554	1878	246	2240
1990-91	1455	152	1126	308	1399
1991-92	473	49	1287	287	1315
1992-93	1311	00	1877	295	2243
1993-94	1999	107	1690	427	2011
1994-95	221	53	557	470	714
1995-96	177	000	708	462	869
1996-97	000	000	624	409	1273
1997-98	446	000	1111	266	1273
1998-99	484	000	1003	141	1213
1999-00	1043	000	1044	123	1259

Source: Records of the union.

Table 2.13

Progress in Health Care Facilities at Chittoor Milk Union, 1988-00

Sl.	Particulars	1987-88	1988-89	1989-90	1990-91	1991-92	1992-93	1993-94	1994-95	1995-96	1996-97	1997-98	1998-99	1999-00
1.	A.I. centres	18	20	52	54	56	73	76	65	50	50	54	50	50
2.	AI done	1226	8357	27856	39204	42016	41068	30067	43646	43809	22488	35576	49103	46581
3.	Animals found pregnant	925	6545	22190	31246	32849	38628	26102	34916	33566	18679	19159	10486	12254
4.	Animals verified	702	3817	16472	29758	31911	35658	22374	26187	28575	16377	17046	21045	25753
5.	Calves born	260	1374	5765	11397	12739	11816	15737	16574	14328	9759	9949	11365	15435
6.	FMD vaccinations	11480	5650	7870	10450	24250	25760	34710	35400	40500	42360	38500	40300	22375
7.	Cattle insured	NA	250	750	1025	10714	5386	2135	120	100	125	86	86	3296
8.	Sterility camps conducted	NA	50	40	32	65	100	36	32	12	10	10	132	182
9.	Cattlefeed sold) (tonnes	NA	1250	2450	5500	7500	4287	2151	860	335	985	740	915	475
10.	Calves dewormed	NA	9750	10500	12500	12000	11420	5360	7314	7811	4250	9428	11185	10500
11.	First aid	NA	750	1050	1550	2500	3630	2268	1950	1921	1007	1120	289	600

Source: Records of the union.

Growth in selected indicators of Chittoor milk union is presented in Table 2.14. There is a sharp and steady decline in almost all indicators considered in the study and it is mainly due to emergence of private dairies in the district. Heritage is one such private dairy which is eating into the progress of Chittoor union. As a result, capacity utilisation of the union declined from 98% in 1990-91 to 41% in 1998-99. Across various unions, Chittoor has the highest (17%) number of DCSs in the state. As regards membership in DCSs, it occupied 3rd position after Guntur and Vijaya Visakha. The district stood first in procurement of milk/society. Thus, on the basis of above three parameters, Chittoor milk union is better than her counterparts in the state (Table 2.3).

Table 2.14

Growth in Selected Indicators of Chittoor Milk Union, 1991-00

Year	*DCSs*	*Milk suppliers (lakhs)*	*Average procure-ment/day (lakh litres)*	*Average sales/day (lakh litres)*	*Capacity utilisa-tion (%)*	*Number of employees*
1990-91	735	0.78	1.97	0.05	98	730
1991-92	822	0.53	1.88	0.06	90	731
1992-93	890	0.67	1.88	0.09	94	731
1993-94	767	0.45	1.47	0.12	74	699
1994-95	586	0.32	0.75	0.10	37	704
1995-96	563	0.25	0.61	0.12	39	668
1996-97	545	0.54	0.63	0.11	31	690
1997-98	444	0.38	0.67	0.10	42	748
1998-99	429	0.42	0.80	0.10	41	646
1999-00						

Source: Records of APDDCF.

Integration of Rural Women into Dairying

To improve socio-economic status of rural women through dairying a pilot project was formulated (1983) with financial assistance of Ford Foundation. Ten women extension supervisors (graduates) in the age group of 20-24 years were selected. Field training was provided in oganisation of societies, conducting surveys for milk-potential, motivation of women milk producers, enrolment of women members, registration of DCSs, training on technical inputs, etc. The following incentives were provided to WDCSs under this project: (i) loans to women belonging to landless are provided @ six members/society, (ii) TV set for each society was subsidised under education programme, (iii) SC and ST members of the society were provided a stainless steel bucket/pail for clean milk production, and (iv) calf feed was supplied on 50% cost to female crossbred calves for a period of six months to acquaint them of scientific feeding of calves for rapid growth and good health. In all, 110 WDCSs with 9360 members were organised under this scheme. Ten women extension workers were employed to guide and promote such WDCSs under Ford Foundation. Once the assistance was withdrawn, the project failed to maintain sustainability as members looked forward for external assistance.

Rural Health

Realising the need for women and child care besides environmental and personal hygiene, Ford Foundation had sanctioned a scheme in which a team of 4 medical officers (two male and two female) along with 4 para medical staff headed by a project director to tour WDCSs, render medical help, and impart medical education to members. Under this programme an educated rural health worker was also identified in each society and trained in first aid, and to cater to minor ailments. Adequate medical services/medicines were also made available with local PHCs. Patients were referred to government headquarters hospital and also to Christian Medical College hospital, Vellore, when necessary. Establishment of 25 libraries in WDCSs were taken up with financial assistance from Rajiv Gandhi Technological Foundation.

Cattle Insurance

Milch cattle belonging to producers of these societies are insured with concessional rate of premium for a period of two years. The premium was divided into three parts: 1/3rd each was borne by union, WDCS, and producer. Each producer was given maximum of two animals for inclusion in insurance programme. In all, 17386 milch cows were insured under this project.

Women Dairy Project under STEP

WDCSs were taken up in V. Kota, Medanapalle, Piler, and Chittoor areas. So far 60 WDCSs were organised with 2921 members in these areas. As an incentive, on an average, each WDCS was given Rs. 1.80 lakhs for sustainability (Table 2.15). Milk equipment accounted for as much as 59% and the rest devoted to human resources development. 30 more societies are proposed to be taken up in 2000-01, last year of the programme. Total estimated cost of this project is Rs. 1.53 crores and rural women dairy association is selected Chittoor district as an NGO to implement this project.

Warangal Milk Union

Warangal district lies between latitude 170-191 and 180-361 north, and longitude 780-491 and 800-431 east. It is bounded on north by Karimnagar; Medak on west; Nalgonda on south; and Khammam on east and south-east. Warangal district had historical and political influences of Kakatiya period (1260-1422), and Asisjahi (1725-1948) and is located in telangana region of Andhra Pradesh. Geographical area of the district is 12,846 sq. kms. consisting of 50 revenue mandals. Of the total geographical area, about 29% is under forests. The district has 28.18 lakh population with 219 persons/sq.km. Major of sources of irrigation in the district are tanks [Ramappa, Ghanpur (m), Pakhal, Lakhnavaram, and Salivagu]. Rice and maize are the major crops and commercial crops like tobacco, and chillies are spreading these days. There are 13 veterinary hospitals, 77 livestock supervisory units, 120 rural livestock units and a polyclinic in the district.

Table 2.15

Assistance under STEP

Sl.No.	*Item*	*Rs. lakhs/WDCS*
1.	Milking equipment	1.07
2.	Animal health care	0.28
3.	HRD	0.28
4.	Support to staff	0.04
5.	Legal literacy	0.13
	Total	1.80

Source: Records of the union.

Table 2.16

Trends in Livestock Population (lakhs) in Warangal, 1983-98

Sl. No.	*Particulars*	*1983*	*1987*	*1993*	*1998*
1	Cattle	9.13	8.59	7.35	6.73
	(a) Males over 3 years	3.26	3.79	3.91	3.77
	(b) Females over 3 years	3.11	2.37	1.91	1.4
	(c) Young stock	2.76	2.43	1.53	1.56
2	Buffaloes	3.6	3.7	4.16	4.1
	(a) Males over 3 years	0.50	0.49	0.35	0.12
	(b) Females over 3 years	1.57	1.65	1.91	1.98
	(c) Young stock	1.53	1.55	1.9	2
3	Sheep	3.26	3.28	4.34	5.54
4	Goats	2.49	2.32	2.57	2.64
5	Poultry	14.98	17.21	19.71	28.87

Source: District statistical hand book.

Warangal dairy was started in 1969 under Integrated Milk Project covering Karimnagar district. Later, it was upgraded as a regional dairy covering Warangal, Khammam, Karimnagar, Nalgonda, and Adilabad with head office at Warangal. As the project is outside the operation flood area, integrated dairy development project was initiated during 1991-96 and efforts made to promote dairy industry in the area.

Table 2.17

Progress in Membership of Warangal Milk Union, 1986-00

Year	*DCSs*	*Membership*		
		Men	*Women*	*Total*
1985-86	07	813	12	825
1986-87	11	1198	20	1217
1987-88	13	1290	22	1312
1988-89	33	2890	174	3064
1989-90	34	3001	178	3179
1990-91	34	3001	373	3374
1991-92	53	4127	1078	5205
1992-93	69	5347	1340	6687
1993-94	79	6092	1378	7470
1994-95	141	9563	2466	12029
1995-96	168	11047	2614	13661
1996-97	178	11847	2948	14795
1997-98	178	11847	2948	14795
1998-99	193	12902	3722	16624
1999-00	234	14715	3988	18703

Source: Records of the union.

Livestock population for 1983-98 is provided in Table 2.16. There is substantial decline in all categories of cattle while marginal increase noticed in buffalo population. Thus, there is a net decrease in bovine population over the 15 years considered. Contrary to this, population of sheep, goats, and poultry has increased, more so with poultry. This indicates that farmers are tilting towards smaller animals mainly due to non-availability of water, feeds, health care, and other support services.

Number of DCSs increased from seven in 1985-86 to 234 in 1999-00. As many as 18703 farmer members are involved in these DCSs. Women constitute 21% of the total membership (Table 2.17). Growth in WDCSs is given in Table 2.18 and there are as many as 33 WDCSs in the milk union. Most of them are located in Jangaon MCC and are organised under STEP programme.

Table 2.18

Progress in All Women DCSs, 1986-00

Year	*All women DCSs*	*Membership*
1985-86	00	00
1986-87	00	00
1987-88	00	00
1988-89	02	100
1989-90	02	100
1990-91	04	295
1991-92	08	897
1992-93	11	1293
1993-94	11	1293
1994-95	14	1510
1995-96	14	1510
1996-97	14	1510
1997-98	19	1764
1998-99	32	2432
1999-00	33	2517

Source: Records of the union.

Trends in milk procurement, sales, turnover, and net profit/ net loss are provided in Table 2.19. Milk procurement increased from 15.98 lakh litres/annum in 1981-82 to 68.67 lakh litres/ annum in 1999-00 while that of sales from 26.34 lakh litres/ annum to 26.80 lakh litres/annum. Surplus milk is sent to Hyderabad main dairy. No trend is observed in the indicators considered. There are ups and downs in these indicators. The unions has been in profits since 1991-92.

Table 2.19

Trends in Milk Procurement and Sales (lakh litres)

Year	*Procurement*	*Sales*	*Turnover (Rs. lakhs)*	*Net profit/net) loss (Rs.lakhs*
1981-82	15.98	26.34	NA	NA
1982-83	35.40	22.24	NA	NA
1983-84	16.17	23.80	NA	NA
1984-85	15.50	25.56	NA	NA
1985-86	32.42	22.59	305.79	5.45
1986-87	30.16	34.26	289.53	-15.49
1987-88	24.62	43.75	315.20	-26.79
1988-89	13.73	41.94	327.29	-41.29
1989-90	13.35	36.71	323.54	-16.70
1990-91	21.68	34.89	209.18	-5.68
1991-92	33.82	33.69	237.98	3.76
1992-93	42.32	31.96	244.67	10.24
1993-94	62.01	32.30	281.96	18.36
1994-95	50.60	39.87	347.59	13.19
1995-96	47.20	36.96	355.04	17.33
1996-97	44.90	25.58	261.36	15.79
1997-98	69.21	21.37	249.86	27.41
1998-99	76.91	20.41	271.76	38.24
1999-00	68.67	26.80	301.51	45.35

Source: Records of the union.

Table 2.20
Unit-wise Procurement (lakh litres)

Year	*Warangal*	*Jangaon*	*Thorrur*	*Mulug*	*Narasapur*	*Total*
1989-90	6.50	0.00	3.97	2.88	0.00	13.35
1990-91	8.74	0.00	6.62	6.32	0.00	21.68
1991-92	13.54	0.00	8.76	11.52	0.00	33.82
1992-93	18.74	0.00	13.74	9.84	0.00	42.32
1993-94	13.19	32.99	9.31	6.52	0.00	62.01
1994-95	11.27	29.42	5.92	3.99	0.00	50.60
1995-96	8.77	28.04	5.71	4.68	0.00	47.20
1996-97	7.52	27.63	4.49	5.35	0.00	44.99
1997-98	14.66	40.07	5.98	8.50	0.00	69.21
1998-99	14.42	46.32	8.49	7.68	0.00	76.91
1999-00	9.30	45.48	7.93	4.66	1.30	68.67

Source: Records of the union.

Data on procurement, as provided in Table 2.19, are the sum totals of five MCCs (Warangal, Jangaon, Thorrur, Mulug, and Narasapur) of the union. MCC-wise procurement is shown in Table 2.20. Though Jangaon MCC started late, it is contributing as much as 2/3rd s of union's total procurement. Status of these MCCs is given in Table 2.21. Warangal is the oldest MCC in the area. Of the total 229 DCSs, 126 DCSs are located in Jangaon area. Apart from DCSs, there are 104 milk producers associations who are not registered bodies and thus have no voting rights in elections to the union. Milk collection, as mentioned earlier, is the highest in Jangaon MCC. The union has 105 regular employees and 60 temporary workers on its rolls.

The union has been manufacturing butter milk, sterilized flavoured milk, and ghee from sour milk. The progress in the production of these products is presented in Table 2.22. It has manufactured 35.3 tonnes of ghee, 2716 litres of flavoured milk, and 31502 litres of butter milk is 1999-00 which is sold in its parlours. Growth in the selected indicators of the union is presented in Table 2.23 and it is self explanatory. Relative position of selected unions and the APDDCF is presented in Table 2.24. Chittoor has more DCSs with low percentage of milk suppliers (20%) and maximum number of employees. Procurement-wise Prakasam is marginally better than Chittoor, and Warangal stood third in that order. As of capacity utilization, all the selected unions reported lesser utilization compare to state average (44%).

Table 2.21

Status of Various MCCs of Warangal Milkshed

Sl. No.	*Particulars*	*Warangal*	*Jangaon*	*Thorrur*	*Mulug*	*Total*
1.	Date of establishment	10.03.69	04.04.93	23.09.80	10.09.71	---
2.	Plant capacity (litres/day)	25000	20000	6000	10000	61000
3.	Milk routes	5	7	4	4	20
4.	No. of DCSs	53	126	28	22	229
5.	No. of MPACs	27	17	29	31	104
6.	Mandals covered	14	9	10	8	41
7.	Milk producers	5910	8070	4120	3245	21345
8.	All women MPCS	4	25	4	6	39
9.	Share capital (Rs. lakhs)	1.71	2.17	0.625	0.36	4.865
10.	No. of village wherein CBCs distributed	18	36	13	12	79
11.	No. of CBCs	360	590	323	416	1,689
12.	Maximum milk procurement (litres/day) (1998-99)	7500	25000	5000	3500	41000
13.	No. of employees	65	23	8	9	105

Source: Records of the union.

WDP under STEP was started in 1997-98 with a target of 40 WDCSs under Jangaon MCC. World Vision of India is associated with the WDP in the district. World Vision of India conducted initial field surveys, identified the target group members, and helped in formation of societies. While selecting members, preference was given to DWCRA members of Ghanapur (L), Devuruppala, and Raghunatapally mandals with 2-3 years of experience. Implementation of the project was started in March 1998.

Table 2.22

Progress in Production of Milk Products, 1986-00

Year	*Butter milk (litres)*	*SF milk (litres)*	*Ghee (kgs)*
1985-86	17570	6344	28500
1986-87	18506	4734	35142
1987-88	24300	2690	24073
1988-89	54793	2504	13627
1989-90	24964	2666	18977
1990-91	20532	2010	21023
1991-92	19487	2440	37449
1992-93	17541	5260	14713
1993-94	12064	4961	27079
1994-95	9156	4796	28421
1995-96	12175	1822	000
1996-97	8331	1500	10792
1997-98	18209	1638	11915
1998-99	2706	4480	29411
1999-00	31502	2716	35342

Source: Records of the union.

Realising the importance breeding, dairy distributed as many as 15 murrah bulls in WDCSs. Selected societies were given assistance in the form of management subsidy, feed subsidy, furniture and equipment, loans for purchasing animals, etc. Chairpersons, secretaries, and testers of these societies were given training in day to day management of the society. Programmes on gender sensitization, health care, nutrition, etc. too were organised in the villages.

Table 2.23

Growth in Selected Indicators of Warangal Milk Union, 1991-00

Year	*DCS*	*Milk suppliers (lakhs) (akhs litres)*	*Average procure-ment/day litres)*	*Average sales/ day (lakh*	*Capacity utilisa-tion (%)*	*Number of employees*
1990-91	20	0.08	0.06	0.10	30	117
1991-92	29	0.18	0.09	0.09	36	132
1992-93	64	0.20	0.12	0.09	42	132
1993-94	152	0.18	0.17	0.09	33	129
1994-95	174	0.18	0.14	0.11	24	149
1995-96	197	0.15	0.13	0.10	23	118
1996-97	174	0.11	0.12	0.07	23	168
1997-98	189	0.17	0.19	0.06	35	133
1998-99	209	0.21	0.21	0.05	37	132
1999-00						

Source: Records of APDDCF.

Summary

Andhra Pradesh is one of the largest states of southern India. Organised dairying was taken up in the early 1960s and initially the responsibility rested with a number of organisations. APDDCF was formed in 1981. It has nine milk unions (Visakha, Godavari, Krishna, Guntur, Prakasam, Nellore, Chittoor, Kurnool, and Nalgonda and Ranga Reddy) and dairies at Anantapur, Mahboobnagar, Medak and Nizamabad, Warangal, and Karimnagar are under its direct control. Indo-Swiss project,

Ford Foundation project, The Netherlands project, and NDDBs CD program were implemented in the state for involving women into mainstream dairying. STEP programme is also being implemented since 1997-98. Of the three selected milk unions for the study, Prakasam represents coastal Andhra, Chittoor falls in Rayalaseema, while Warangal is drawn from Telangana region.

Table 2.24

Relative Position of Selected Milk Unions on the Basis of Important Indictors, 2000

Sl. No.	*Indicator*	*Prakasam*	*Chittoor*	*Warangal*	*Andhra Pradesh*
1.	DCS	344	429	209	4270*
2	Membership	79186	66290	14495	773203
3.	Milk suppliers	27653	13500	12122	182268
4.	Milk chilling centres	4	5	4	63
5.	Average procurement/ day (lakh litres)	0.83	0.80	0.21	8.95
6.	Average sales/day (lakh litres)	0.17	0.10	0.06	6.62
7.	Capacity utilisation (%)	28	41	37	44
8.	Number of employees	229	646	132	7132

* Almost equal number of milk producers association centres are also supplying milk at all levels.

Source: Records of APDDCF.

Prakasam is one of the backward districts of Andhra Pradesh. Majority of the milk producers in the district are landless agricultural labourers, marginal, and small farmers. The milk union was organised in 1986 with an installed capacity of 80000 litres/day which was further expanded to 3.50 lakh litres/day. The union has 426 DCSs, and 355 milk producers association centres covering 1.06 milk producer members. Capacity utilization of the union is the lowest in the state. Half of the DCSs and the management of the union were superceded in 1999. A member of a private dairies had come up in the district, and union is unable to complete with them. Milk payments were due and, members are unhappy with the union. Women dairy project was taken up in the Markapur division of the district. There are 45 WDCSs with a membership of 1691.

Chittoor is known for its small holdings and crossbred population. Ford Foundation aided women development project was implemented during 1983-87. About 110 WDCSs were organised under this project, but currently most of them are either closed or dysfunctional. The union had its golden period during early 1990s and its average procurement/day was about 2.05 lakh litres during 1991. There has been a steep fall over years and currently hovering around 71000 litres/day (1999-00). Milk payments were pending for 2-3 months, when the researcher visited the union in July 2000. Emergence of private dairies, casual nature of elected management, inappropriate marketing strategies, and non-cooperation from the employees made producer members to turn towards private dairies.

Warangal district falls outside the operation flood area and thus was developed under Integrated Dairy Development Project of NCDC. There are about 230 DCSs in the milk shed with a total membership of 18703. It has four MCCs with an installed capacity of 61000 litres/day (1999-00). As the local sales were very low, about 75% of its procurement goes to Hyderabad main dairy and it is posting profits for the last 9 years. WDCSs under STEP programme were taken up in Jangaon area of the milk shed.

Chapter 3

Profiles of KMF and Selected Unions

An attempt is made in this chapter to analyse performance of KMF and selected milk unions of Karnataka. Traditional performance indicators like membership, procurement, sales, production of milk products, input services extended, turnover, profits/losses, etc., are considered for this purpose.

Introduction

Karnataka has written history of more than 2,000 years. Apart from its being subjected to the rule of Nandas, Mauryas, and Shatavahanas, Karnataka came to have indigenous dynasties like Kadambas of Banavasi and Gangas. The Rashtrakutas (753-973 AD) or Malkhed who succeeded Chalukyas levied tribute on the rulers of Kanauj in the so-called 'Age of imperial Kanauj'. Kannada literature developed during this period. Outstanding Jain scholars of India lived in their court. Vijayanagar empire (1336-1646) fostered indigenous tradition and encouraged arts, religion and literature in Sanskrit, Kannada, Telugu and Tamil. Overseas trade flourished. The Bahamani Sultans and Bijapur Adilshahis raised fine Indo-Saracenci buildings and encouraged Urdu and Persian literature. Advent of the Portuguese resulted in introduction of new crops (tobacco, maize, chillies, groundnut, potato, etc.). After the fall of the Peshwa (1818) and Tipu Sultan (1799), Karnataka came under the British. Christian missionaries introduced English education and printing during the 19th century. Revolution in transport, communication and industries was evidenced. Urban middle class emerged. Mysore dynasty helped industrialisation and cultural growth. Freedom movement was followed by movement for unification of Karnataka. After independence, new united Mysore State was created in 1956 and was renamed as Karnataka in 1973.

It has 320 kms coastline (Arabian Sea) on west; Goa and Maharashtra on north and north-west; Andhra Pradesh on east; Tamil Nadu on south-east; and Kerala on south-west. The irrigation potential of the state from all sources has been estimated as about ha. 55 lakhs consisting of ha. 35 lakhs under major and medium, and ha. 20 lakhs under minor irrigation (1997-98). Agriculture and allied activities account for nearly 65% of the work force in the state. Rice is the main food crop followed by maize, millets, and pulses. Horticulture crops are grown in an area of ha. 18 lakhs with an annual production of 124 lakh tonnes valued at Rs. 6000 crore (1998-99). The area under forests is ha. 30.62 which constitutes about 20.10% of the total geographical area. Cattle breeding is important in far south. Mysore Prince Hyder Ali bred fast-trotting bullocks for use in warfare at the end of 1700's.

Organised Dairying in Karnataka

An integrated project was launched in June, 1974 to restructure and reorganise dairy industry on cooperative principles in the state. Karnataka Dairy Development Corporation was set up in 1974 to implement World Bank aided dairy development project. Initially the project covered 8 southern districts of Karnataka. This multilevel, multiunit organisation with total vertical integration was set up with DCSs at grass root level, milk unions at the district level, and a Dairy Development Corporation at the state level, vested with responsibility of implementing Rs. 51 crore project. Thus, the first DCS was organised on November 20, 1975. At the end of September 1984, World Bank aided project ended and the dairy development activities continued under Operation Flood-II. Karnataka Cooperative Milk Producers' Federation Limited (KMF) came into existence in May 1984 as a successor to KDDC.

After the closure of Operation Flood-II (1986), dairy development activities continued under Operation Flood-III which ended on 31.3.96. Since then, spill over works are financed by NDDB under different terms and conditions.

Objectives of KMF

KMF is a cooperative apex body representing dairy farmers organisations and also implementing dairy development activities in the state. Major objectives of the KMF are: (a) to provide assured and remunerative market for milk produced by farmer members, (b) to supply quality milk to urban consumers, (c) to build village level institutions in cooperative sector to manage dairy activities, (d) to ensure provision of milk production enhancement inputs, processing facilities and dissemination of know how, and (e) to facilitate rural development by providing opportunities for self employment at village level, preventing migration to urban areas, introducing cash economy and opportunity for steady income.

Status of KMF

A network of 8235 dairy DCSs have been organised (1999) and are spread over 166 talukas of 27 districts. These societies were organised into 13 milk unions. There are 37 chilling centres, 3 farm coolers, 17 liquid milk plants, and 2 product dairies. Two cattle feed plants of 100 TPD capacity each and one plant of 200 TPD capacity with mineral mixture production facility are also functioning. Bull breeding farm and frozen semen bank (Hassarghatta) has been established and is well stocked with exotic quality high pedigree bulls. Further, a central training institute (Bangalore) and 3 regional training centres (Mysore, Dharwad, and Gulbarga) are functioning along with three diagnostic laboratories. Besides this, it has a Mother Dairy (Yalahanka), and Nandini Milk Products Factory (Bangalore). Under Technology Mission on Dairy Development project, it was envisaged to distribute liquid nitrogen which is required to store semen straws. Six silos of 10,000 litres capacity each were erected at Bangalore, Mysore, Gulbarga, Dharwad, Hassan, and Shimoga with a total cost of Rs. 3.0 crores.

The average procurement of milk touched a peak of 17.79 lakh litres/day in November, 1998. Liquid milk sales was at 14.42 lakh litres/day (1999). The sale of cattle feed was 86,371 tonnes during 1998-99. The turnover of the organisation was Rs. 869.85 crores (1998-99).

The present level of activities encompass about 15.22 lakhs of dairy farmers as primary members. Of these, 1.50 lakhs are SCs, 0.87 are STs, and 2.88 are women members. A total of about 5500 employees are working in various capacities in all the units of KMF and affiliated milk unions. The indirect employment generated through various project activities of veterinary services, milk transportation through trucks and tankers, milk sales through agents, parlours, booths, etc., is around 37,000. About 14,000 persons are employed as village level functionaries in the DCSs.

Role of DCS

Dairy cooperative society is a basic organisation functioning at village level. Democracy is practiced in these societies which are organised on cooperative principles. Local leadership is promoted by training local people to organise and manage activities, and village level institution building. All milch animal owners are eligible to become members of dairy cooperative societies. The DCS functions as a marketing outlet for milk produced in the village. Input facilities are also channelised to dairy farmers through these societies which include veterinary first aid, sale of cattle feed, supply of fodder seeds, seedlings, provision of mobile and emergency veterinary health cover, dissemination of know how, etc. Payment for the milk purchased is also arranged through the society. A string of DCSs is organised to form a milk procurement route linked to chilling centre or a dairy.

Role of Milk Union

Union is the middle tier of the network. Unions are formed by federating societies in earmarked geographical area. The milk unions are organised to make them economically viable and jurisdiction extends normally from one district to three districts. There are 5 milk unions whose jurisdiction covers a single district, four unions cover 2 districts each, 3 unions cover 3 districts, and one union's territory extends to 4 districts. All unions own their milk processing facilities.

The unions organise new DCSs, assist DCSs in management (audit of accounts, supervision, purchase, process, and market liquid milk). Provision of input facilities are also organised by union and channelised to dairy farmers through DCSs. The input facilities include supply of cattle feed, fodder, AI, veterinary services, training and know how on scientific animal husbandry, etc.

Role of Federation

The main aim of the federation is to market surplus milk and milk products, under a common brand name, and to produce and supply centralised inputs. Mother Diary and Nandini Milk Products at Bangalore are under the control of KMF. Four cattle feed plants, a bull breeding farm and frozen semen bank, a central training institute, and a centralised testing and quality control laboratory are functioning under the direct control of KMF. Coordination of activities between the unions and developing market for increasing milk production is the responsibility of KMF. Local milk market in the area of union is being looked after by respective unions. Surpluses and deficiencies of liquid milk amongst member milk unions are managed by federation. The major quantity of the milk is sold as liquid milk. Products like butter, ghee, SMP, WMP peda, flavoured milk, burfi, paneer jamoon mix, jamoons, mysorepak and ice cream are also manufactured and sold. The products are sold under the brand name of 'Nandini'. Marketing of liquid milk and products outside the state is organised by the federation. Excellence in quality is maintained to lay a solid foundation for widespread acceptance of Nandini products. This will ensure an assured market for the ever increasing milk production. Balanced cattle feed, bypass cattle feed, mineral mixture, frozen semen straws and liquid nitrogen are produced by the federation and supplied to the unions.

Progress of the Federation

As mentioned above, KMF has 13 milk unions, with a total registered DCSs of 8469. Of the total functional DCSs, 1221 are defunct. It has 14.89 lakh membership of which 22% are pourer members (Table 3.1). Bangalore and Kolar milk unions have majority of the DCSs and membership in the federation. Progress of KMF is measured in terms of DCSs formed, membership (both men and women), milk procurement, and turnover (Table 3.2). There is a study period increase in all parameters considered during the study period. DCSs increased from 3233 in 1985-86 to 8235 in 1998-99 and that of membership from 7.17 lakhs to 15.23 lakhs during the same period. Women constituted 14% of the total membership in 1987-88 and it increased to 19% by 1998-99 and turnover from Rs. 90 crores in 1985-86 to Rs. 870 crores in 1998-99.

Table 3.1

Status of Functional Societies at KMF, 2000

Union	*Registered*	*Commi-ssioned*	*Functional*	*Defunct*	*Total Members*	*Pourers*
Bangalore	1271	1233	1203	30	193142	63799
Kolar	1291	1253	1212	41	230877	59807
Mysore	704	693	574	99	179847	35282
Mangalore	695	678	653	25	201583	35763
Tumkur	541	534	452	82	136723	16599
Hassan	661	650	575	75	108161	22547
Dharwad	723	713	520	193	111991	16648
Belgaum	507	498	340	158	56493	14323
Bijapur	306	301	202	99	39265	4520
Gulbarga	308	303	157	146	43843	5536
Dakshin Kannada	339	339	331	8	57620	21679
Shimoga	734	719	591	128	87306	19634
Raichur	389	385	248	137	41847	9077
Total	8469	8299	7078	1221	1488698	328214

Source: Records of the KMF.

Table 3.2

Progress in Membership, 1986-00

Year	*DCSs*	*Membership (lakhs)*			*Procurement*	*Turnover*
		Men	*Women*	*Total*	*(million kgs)*	*(Rs. crores)*
1985-86	3233	N.A.	N.A.	N.A.	N.A.	89.97
1986-87	3979	N.A.	0.80	N.A.	N.A.	161.92
1987-88	4266	6.19	0.98	7.17	302.1	204.11
1988-89	5017	7.10	1.15	8.25	319.1	111.48
1989-90	5446	7.93	1.30	9.23	343.8	237.64
1990-91	5803	8.65	1.46	10.11	334.1	270.96
1991-92	6091	9.43	1.63	11.06	330.8	311.25
1992-93	6426	10.10	1.78	11.88	400.0	377.12
1993-94	6717	10.63	2.00	12.63	430.5	452.84
1994-95	7002	11.11	2.17	13.28	414.3	471.68
1995-96	7346	11.54	2.33	13.87	441.8	535.59
1996-97	7658	12.04	2.51	14.55	513.9	693.12
1997-98	8023	12.33	2.68	15.01	538.0	748.19
1998-99	8235	12.35	2.88	15.23	575.7	869.85
1999-00			2.84			

Source: Same as Table 3.1.

Growth in sale of milk and milk products are provided in Table 3.3. Except in SMP and WMP, production of other three products (milk, butter, and ghee) increased over the study period. District-wise location of WDCSs is provided in Table 3.4. Gulbarga-Bidar milk union has the highest WDCSs (141) while Mysore-Chamarajanagar milk union has highest membership (38254). Average annual procurement ranged between 0.18 lakh litres/day in Bijapur milk union to 4.23 lakh litres/day in Bangalore milk union. Federation, through its unions, provides a number of facilities (Table 3.5). AIs performed, cattlefeed sold, training to employees of DCSs, and farmers trained increased manifold during period under study.

Table 3.3

Growth in Sales of Milk and Milk Products, 1982-00

Year	*Milk (lakh litres)*	*Butter (tonnes)*	*Ghee (tonnes)*	*SMP (tonnes)*	*WMP (tonnes)*
1981-82	915	99	642	00	00
1982-83	990	101	742	00	00
1983-84	1092	127	1111	00	00
1984-85	1186	375	1137	00	00
1985-86	1526	291	1696	9	1
1986-87	1984	251	2931	1504	146
1987-88	2252	250	2314	3672	555
1988-89	2618	269	2757	1439	744
1989-90	2830	468	2738	935	353
1990-91	3231	189	1997	641	555
1991-92	3324	671	2410	85	493
1992-93	3336	1162	3328	742	3
1993-94	3606	3736	5038	2776	17
1994-95	3894	1217	3371	1371	245
1995-96	4138	1535	3646	315	67
1996-97	4496	1928	4752	366	00
1997-98	4748	1386	4379	282	00
1998-99	5065	2642	4730	483	00
1999-00					

Source: Same as Table 3.1.

Table 3.4

District-wise Status of WDCSs in Karnataka

Sl. No.	*District/Union*	*WDCSs*	*Membership*	*Average procurement (lakh litres/ day)*
1.	Bangalore	56	32827	4.23
2.	Kolar	47	35525	3.95
3.	Mysore	64	38254	0.96
4.	Chamarajanagar			
5.	Belgaum	69	7871	0.51
6.	Bijapur	32	8561	0.18
7.	Gulbarga	141	21501	0.20
8.	Bidar			
9.	Dakshina Kannada	38	11187	0.65
10.	Udupi			
11.	Shimoga	116	21335	1.00
12.	Chitradurga			
13.	Raichur	66	11820	0.39
14.	Bellary			
15.	Koppay			
16.	Mandya	48	37180	1.39
17.	Tumkur	41	22464	0.72
18.	Hassan	50	11303	0.93
19.	Coorg			
20.	Chickmagalur			
21.	Dharwad	57	26488	0.66
22.	North Canara			
23.	Gadag			
24.	Haveri			
25.	Total	825	286316	15.77

Source: Same as Table 3.1.

Table 3.5

Progress in Supply of Technical Inputs at KMF, 1986-00

Year	*AIs (lakhs*	*Animals treated*	*Sale of cattlefeed (lakh kgs)*	*DCSs staff trained*	*Farmers trained*
1985-86	23.89	5.67	241	287	487
1986-87	35.08	5.67	369	471	780
1987-88	36.59	5.39	412	390	1009
1988-89	45.69	6.73	472	485	934
1989-90	56.53	7.97	531	677	488
1990-91	59.74	8.43	462	333	722
1991-92	63.54	8.64	424	238	554
1992-93	66.73	9.99	656	588	303
1993-94	68.30	9.72	622	725	523
1994-95	62.80	5.31	534	905	419
1995-96	64.70	2.68	609	1321	6983
1996-97	68.20	2.63	716	2287	3571
1997-98	73.60	3.03	672	3136	4653
1998-99	81.90	3.58	855	1911	4413
1999-00		3.38			

Source: Same as Table 3.1.

STEP Programme at KMF

The details of the STEP programme are provided in Chapter 1 as also in Appendix A. An attempt is made here provide a brief about progress of KMF in implementing STEP programme. A separate division has been created under Project Director (STEP). Core teams are established in all milk unions to implement STEP headed by Core Team Leader who is directly responsible for implementation of STEP in the union's jurisdiction. Trainers training programmes are arranged at the federation and training modules for implementation of socio-economic programmes in DCSs are developed with the assistance of NIPPCID. Periodical review meetings are conducted by Project Director (STEP). The overall monitoring of STEP is being done by a Monitoring Committee constituted specially for STEP and headed by Managing Director of KMF.

Benchmark surveys conducted and WDCSs made functional by the core team. Apart from implementation of economic activity (dairying) socio-economic activities envisaged under STEP are implemented with the help NGOs/ government departments/independent resource persons of eminence drawn from different walks of life. Target group members of 15-20 are motivated to form self help groups to successfully organise micro level thrift and savings with credit inflow for dairy development activities.

Table 3.6

Assistance (rupees) to WDCS under STEP

Assistance	*Amount (rupees)*
Propulsion changes	3500
Equipment	6000
Furniture	12000
Milk cans	7200
Share capital	5000
Managerial grant	9800
Margin money	37500
First aid box	1500
Medicines	1000
Total	83500

Source: Same as Table 3.1.

For the purpose of STEP, the state is divided into two zones. Zone-I comprises of Bangalore, Hassan, Kolar, Mandya, Tumkur, and Mysore. Zone-II includes Bellary, Belgaum, Bijapur, Dakshina Kannada, Dharwar, Gulbarga, and Shimoga. 20,000 rural women below the poverty line have been identified in groups of 50 from 400 WDCSs throughout the state. Total project outlay is Rs. 9.89 crores including 10% contribution of participating milk unions. The project was started in October, 1997 and was expected to be completed by March, 2000. It was extended till 2001 and Government. of India announced (February 2001) further extension of this program for another three years to organise 200 WDCSs and an amount of Rs. 6.35 crores was sanctioned. The approximate expenditure/member is Rs. 4800 and Rs. 0.84 lakh/ WDCS (Table 3.6).

Table 3.7

Progress of STEP at KMF (December, 2000)

Sl.No.	*Particulars*	*Zone-I*	*Zone-II*	*Total*
1.	WDCSs registered	205	195	400
2.	Total members	25024	17337	42361
3.	Members supplying milk	6774	4672	11446
4.	Average procurement/ WDCS/day (in ltrs)	157	93	125
5.	AI centres established	43	43	86
6.	AIs done	2296	1938	4234
7.	Cattlefeed sales (tonnes)	2737	2684	5431
8.	Secretaries trained	159	142	301
9.	Gender sensitization	63	46	109
10.	Members participated	4266	2529	6795
11.	Health and nutrition programmes	170	134	304
12.	Members participated	12399	7898	20297
13.	Legal literacy programmes	169	131	300
14.	Members participated	10531	6784	17315
15.	SHGs formed	269	240	509
16.	SHG deposits (Rs. lakhs)	19.51	11.95	31.46
17.	Animals purchased	709	874	1583
18.	Sanitary latrines	286	0	286

Source: Same as Table 3.1.

So far 400 WDCSs were registered with a membership of about 42000. Of these 41000, 17920 were identified as target group (marginalised, assetless rural women, and urban poor) and their performance is being monitored continuously. Progress under STEP is given in Table 3.7. Currently

(December, 2000) 32% of the target group members are supplying milk to WDCSs with an average supply 1.18 litres/ day. In all, 30 million litres of milk was procured from these 370 WDCSs in 1998-99. There are 86 AI centres and 131 first aid centres in these WDCSs. Training programmes are being conducted for secretaries, testers, committee members, and producers. KMF produced an hour long telefilm 'Sangavvan Kathe' highlighting objectives of STEP. In addition to these facilities, WDCSs are paid a commission of 25 paise/litre of milk collected, 10 paise/testing, 50 paise/litre towards transportation, Rs. 125/milch animal insurance, Rs. 450/milch animal purchased, etc. A state level seminar on women dairy cooperatives was organised at Bangalore in February, 2001 to review a progress of the project. Around 2000 women from these WDCSs participated and shared their experiences at the seminar.

Formation of Self Help Groups (SHGs)

SHGs aims at providing loans to poor women for starting self-employment. It was proposed to start a SHG in each WDCS with 15-20 women members. Selected women are helped to avail of loans from Rashtriya Mahila Kosh and NABARD. WDCSs and SHGs helped rural women to become self reliant and come out of shadow of their husbands. They made them realise 'their power within their self' to shake off clutches of bondage.

Raichur and Bellary Districts Cooperative Milk Producers Societies Union Limited

Raichur and Bellary milk union was organised in 1989. Prior to registering the union, there was a milk chilling centre (MCC) under the control of KMF. Subsequently, all assets and liabilities of MCC were transferred to union. The area of operation of the milk union consists of 16 talukas from Bellary, Koppal, and Raichur districts. In all there are about 1913 villages in these districts of which 474 are covered by now through 386 primary dairy cooperative societies (DCSs). Of the 386 DCSs, 1/3rd are defunct. Presently, average procurement/day/DCS is hovering around 130 litres and 90 DCSs are procuring less than 100 litres/ day. There are as many as 85 DCSs under the jurisdiction of the milk union where migrant Andhra people settled. These villages are locally called as 'camps' and they contribute as much as 1/3rd of the total union procurement. These people came to Bellary in the early 50s when irrigation network was created here. They were the first to cultivate paddy, chillies, cotton etc. crops in the area and simultaneously, developed dairy industry too in the district.

Table 3.8

Breedable Bovine Population (lakhs), 2000

Details	*Raichur*	*Bellary*	*Koppal*	*Total*
Crossbreds	0.06	0.06	0.07	0.19
Local cows	0.63	0.74	0.45	1.82
Buffaloes	0.70	0.86	0.53	2.09
Total	1.39	1.66	1.05	4.01
Milk production (lakh litres/day)	1.40	1.34	1.27	3.71
Productivity (litres/day)	1.010	0.810	1.210	0.935

Source: Records of the union.

The union has an elected board with 11 Board of Directors of which six are elected members. Milk union has 4.01 lakhs breedable bovine population (Table 3.8) of which only 0.19 lakh are crossbreds. Average productivity of these animals is worked out at 0.935 litres/day. Upgradation of buffaloes and crossbreeding in cows holds key in improving productivity. Further, availability of green fodder, health care facilities, herd management, etc. go a long way in this context. Per capita consumption of milk/day is the highest (258 ml.) in Koppal district followed by Raichur (208 ml.), and Bellary (169 ml.) Thus, there is considerable scope to increase milk consumption in Bellary and Raichur districts.

Table 3.9

Progress in Membership at Raichur and Bellary Milk Union, 1991-00

Year	*Registered DCSs*	*Functional DCSs*	*Membership Men*	*Membership Women*	*Total*
1990-91	200	171	18168	3832	22000
1991-92	219	212	23077	4923	28000
1992-93	256	218	27408	5592	33000
1993-94	278	235	29883	7117	37000
1994-95	297	212	30481	8519	39000
1995-96	352	243	33310	9690	43000
1996-97	383	264	34549	10451	45000
1997-98	408	277	35773	11227	47000
1998-99	421	295	37195	11805	49000
1999-00	386	255	30180	11820	42000

Source: Records of the union.

Table 3.10

Progress in WDCSs, 1993-00

Year	*All women DCSs*	*Membership*
1992-93	1	65
1993-94	6	382
1994-95	6	582
1995-96	11	842
1996-97	13	1281
1997-98	30	2946
1998-99	39	3948
1999-00	44	4404

Source: Records of the union.

Table 3.11

Chilling Centre-wise Distribution of WDCSs, 2000

Sl. No.	*MCC*	*Women DCSs*	*Membership*
1.	Raichur	1	78
2.	Bellary	3	320
3.	Ittigi	12	1297
4.	Gangavathi	17	1732
5.	Dadesugur	11	977
	Total	44	4404

Source: Records of the union.

Table 3.12

Progress in Procurement and Sales, 1991-00

Year	*Procurement (lakh litres)*	*Sale of milk (lakh litres)*	*Peda (tonnes)*	*Ghee (tonnes)*	*Lassi (000)**	*Curds (000)**	*Butter milk (000)**
1990-91	109.34	66.15	0	0	0	0	0
1991-92	96.47	84.95	0	10.17	0	0	0
1992-93	106.90	86.11	0.058	25.17	0	0	0
1993-94	116.02	99.17	1.0	98.70	0	0	0
1994-95	92.09	92.34	5.41	85.22	0	0	0
1995-96	103.24	117.04	3.44	87.78	13.00	0	0
1996-97	121.83	121.40	3.20	146.97	13.95	0	0
1997-98	133.87	117.79	6.05	173.23	11.17	0	0
1998-99	141.78	119.46	8.00	180.00	15.17	0	0
1999-00	139.59	117.93	5.83	173.76	18.02	6.53	5.58

* in 200 ml. pouches.

Source: Records of the union.

There has been a gradual increase in the number of registered and functional DCSs during 1991-99 which declined in the subsequent year (Table 3.9). Thirty six DCSs were closed permanently during 1999-00. Vast geographical area (22365 sq.kms.) spread over three districts coupled with inadequate milk collection are the major problems of the union. Further, 10 private dairies had also come up in the milkshed who collects about 50000 litres/day. These include Lakshmi Srinivasa (Sindanur), and Durga (Bellary).

Total membership of the union stood at 42000 in 1999-00 of which 28% are women. There are 44 all women DCSs (WDCSs) in the milkshed and majority (31) of these WDCSs were started under the STEP programme of the Government of India. Membership of the 44 WDCSs is 4404 (Table 3.10). These 44 WDCSs are spread over five MCCs of the union (Table 3.11). Out of the 44 WDCSs, 17 are located in Gangavathi MCC (Koppal district) followed by Ittigi (Bellary district).

Progress in procurement, sale of milk, and production of various milk products at the union is provided in Table 3.12. There has been a gradual improvement in procurement of milk during the study period (1991-00). It increased from 109.34 lakh litres/annum to 141.78 lakh litres/annum, giving an average milk procurement of 38844 litres/day in 1998-99 which declined to 38244 litres/day in 1999-00. Further sales of fluid milk increased from 66.15 lakhs litres in 1990-91 to 117.93 lakhs litres/annum in 1999-00. Thus, the union is marketing around 33000 litres/day through 210 agents spread over 45 towns in 1999-00. Excess milk is converted into peda, ghee, lassi, curds, and butter milk. Growth in production of these products can be seen from Table 3.12.

Progress in sales realisations, net profits, and reserve fund is shown in Table 3.13. Sales figures swelled by three folds during the study period and the union posted net profits in six out of nine years considered. Net losses were mainly due to heavy investments in establishing chilling centres at various places in the milkshed and expansion of the main dairy.

Table 3.13
Progress in Sales, Net Profits, and Reserve Fund (Rs. lakhs), 1992-00

Year	*Sales*	*Net profit*	*Reserve fund*
1991-92	407.57	+0.65	0.00
1992-93	734.88	-91.04	0.00
1993-94	1021.05	-78.42	0.00
1994-95	1124.67	+58.08	0.00
1995-96	1162.00	+20.64	0.00
1996-97	1406.38	+116.41	0.00
1997-98	1569.06	+30.75	0.00
1998-99	1746.97	+4.21	20.57
1999-00	1717.07	-103.10	41.64

Source: Records of the union.

Table 3.14
Staff Position, 2000

Section	*Managers*	*Supervisors*	*Technicians*	*Clerks*	*Drivers*	*Workers*	*Total*
P&I	8	25	-	2	-	5	40
Production	1	3	1	-	8	41	54
Engineering	-	3	10	-	-	14	27
QC	-	-	1	-	-	-	1
Purchase & stores	-	1	-	2	-	2	5
MIS	-	-	-	1	-	-	1
Marketing	-	1	-	5	-	11	17
Finance & Accounts	-	1	-	4	-	5	10
Administration	1	1	-	-	2	8	12
MCCs	-	3	2	-	-	26	31
Sub-office	-	-	-	1	-	2	3
Typists	-	-	-	3	-	-	3
Total	10	38	14	18	10	114	204

Source: Records of the union.

The union has 204 employees on its rolls. Section-wise and category-wise break up of the employees is provided in Table 3.14. Maximum number of employees/workers are in the departments of production (54), followed by procurement and inputs (40), and engineering (27).

Union has employed three veterinary doctors and animal health/infertility camps are organised once in six months. In addition, emergency visits are also provided on a nominal charges. Out of 255 DCSs, 72 have artificial insemination (AI) facility. The secretaries of these DCSs are trained for three months in AI and on an average 15 inseminations/month are carried out at these centres. Due to inadequate personnel, infrastructure, etc. AI facility is provided to only 2% of the breedable bovine population in the milkshed. In addition to providing above health care facilities, union has been selling 1400-1500 tonnes/year of balanced cattle feed at no loss no profit basis.

Milk is collected twice daily in almost all the DCSs. However, quality of milk is not tested daily. Testing is carried out only at such DCSs where producers demand it, or where milko-testers are available, or where there is monitoring from members of the management committee or employees of DCSs. As the area is vast and societies are scattered over three districts, it becomes difficult for the union supervisors to oversee the day to day management of the DCSs. Payments are made twice a month. Procurement terribly falls in the months of August/ September and February/March while it touches a peak during May/June and November/December. Of the total milk collected as much as 30% is contributed by buffaloes while the rest is by cows.

The union aims at (a) availability of quality milk round the clock in the market, (b) tapping hotels, jails, hospitals, and other institutional market by improving quality and supply, (c) organising consumer awareness programmes, (d) evolving a system of consumer-agent grievances redressal,

(e) introducing a team concept for market visits, and (f) constituting a core group from quality, plant, and marketing departments to solve day to day problems.

BELGAUM DISTRICT COOPERATIVE MILK PRODUCERS SOCIETIES UNION LIMITED

Historical Background

The district has 1138 villages with a geographical area of 13415 sq.kms. Total population of the district is 29.80 lakhs. Rivers like Krishna, Malaprabha, Ghataprabha, Dudhganga, Vedganga, Markande, and Hiranyakesi irrigate this district. As a result, more than 55% of the total area is irrigated and Belgaum contributed immensely to the green revolution. Subsequently, the district played a significant role in bringing white revolution too in the state. It has Gokak water falls, Renukadevi temple (Soudatti), Someswara temple (Sogal), and Sabari temple near Ramadurg. Freedom fighters like Kittoor Chennamma, Sangolli Rayanna, and Belawadi Mallamma were born in this area.

Belgaum is a border district of Karnataka surrounded by Kolhapur (Maharashtra) and Goa. It has 10 talukas (Attani, Raibag, Chikkodi, Hukkeri, Gokak, Belgaum, Khanapur, Bailhongal, Savadatti, and Ramdurg). The district has a milch animal population of 3.39 lakhs (0.49 lakh cows, 0.19 lakh crossbreds, and 2.73 lakhs buffaloes). Estimated total milk production of the district is 4.70 lakh litres/day of which 2.64 lakh litres/day is marketable surplus. Average yield of milch buffalo is 1.77 litres/day, 1.44 litres/day for cows, and 3.99 litres/day for crossbreds. Due to peculiar qualities, buffalo milk of this district has great demand in Goa and Maharashtra. Belgaum is famous for kunda sweet, a milk based product.

Early Efforts for Dairying

Organised milk procurement was started in the district in 1966 by establishing a 10000 litres/day dairy by Government of Karnataka. It was decided to organise Amul pattern cooperative milk societies in 1983 and first DCS was registered in the same year. Subsequently, government dairy was handed over to KMF in the early part of 1985 and milk union was registered in the end of 1985. By 1988, KMF handed over the expanded dairy (20000 litres/day) to the Belgaum union. The union was taken up under the Operation Flood Programme-III. Funds were provided to expand the dairy up to 60000 litres/day with a cost of Rs. 5.53 crores. It was expected to be completed by 1990. Due to some conflict between NDDB and the contractor, expanded dairy was handed over in 1995. Expecting enhanced installed capacities, management intensified procurement activities, opened new routes, increased input supplies, etc. As a result, procurement reached a peak of 90000 litres/day while the installed capacity was only 20000 litres/day. During the same period union invested huge amounts to start 4000 litres/day bulk cooler at Ramdurg, and 20000 litres/day chilling centre at Gokak. As a result of these consequences, the union incurred a loss of Rs. 3.00 crores during 1992-93 as also lost producers loyalty (milk holidays were declared thrice a week!). Working and other details of the union are presented in the following sections.

Objectives of the Union

The union was organised with the following objectives:

(a) to provide remunerative price to milk producers and supply quality milk to consumers round the year,

(b) to organise primary dairy cooperatives societies at the village level, and

(c) to provide necessary input services to DCSs at reasonable price.

In the year 1983, KMF posted 16 trained employees to replicate Anand pattern cooperative societies in the district. The first milk route of the union was started with 12 DCSs with an average procurement of 500 litres/day.

Progress of the membership, registered and functional DCSs can be noticed from Table 3.15. Registered DCSs increased from 114 in 1985-86 to 504 in 1999-00 while that of functional DCSs increased from 84 to 342 during the same period (about 1/3rd of them are defunct). The union's authorised share capital is Rs. 10 crores of which Rs. 77.06 lakhs is the paid up capital and the entire share capital is contributed by these DCSs only. Producer members increased from 9015 in 1985-86 to 56827 in 1999-00 of which 14% of them are women.

Table 3.15
Progress in Membership at Belgaum Milk Union, 1986-00

Year	*DCSs*		*Membership*		
	Registered	*Functional*	*Men*	*Women*	*Total*
1985-86	114	84	8139	876	9015
1986-87	198	123	14903	1443	16346
1987-88	237	137	23242	1783	25025
1988-89	251	189	26825	1987	28812
1989-90	303	204	32179	2349	34528
1990-91	318	237	31883	7310	39193
1991-92	321	268	38413	7428	45841
1992-93	324	307	44003	7653	51656
1993-94	374	314	45888	8052	53940
1994-95	374	307	48104	8501	56605
1995-96	392	292	49644	8992	58636
1996-97	406	298	51343	9228	60571
1997-98	467	333	54809	9304	64113
1998-99	484	335	64673	9621	74294
1999-00	504	342	48956	7871	56827

Source: Records of the union.

Progress in WDCSs is provided in Table 3.16. In all, there are 55 functional WDCSs with a membership of 6099. Growth in WDCSs during 1986-97 was marginal, however it picked up due to STEP programme of the Government of India. The WDCSs organised under STEP get Rs. 1.25 lakhs to Rs. 1.50 lakhs in the form of milk cans, DCS materials, share capital, management subsidy, furnitures, AI crate, milk testing acids, subsidy on cattle feed, cattle transportation charges, LN2 container, deworming medicines, fodder seeds, margin money, and training. Thus, 42 WDCS were organised under STEP in the district. Initial response from these WDCSs is encouraging. Most of these chairpersons, committee members, secretaries, testers, and few members are trained with the funds available under STEP. The union has a separate milk route called Sabari route exclusively covering WDCSs under Ramadurg MCC. As many as 17 WDCSs were organised under STEP under this MCC.

Table 3.16

Progress in All Women DCSs, 1986-00

Year	*All women DCSs*		*Membership*
	Registered	*Functional*	
1985-86	2	1	60
1986-87	2	1	60
1987-88	2	2	130
1988-89	2	2	136
1989-90	2	2	142
1990-91	2	2	150
1991-92	3	3	206
1992-93	7	6	431
1993-94	7	4	450
1994-95	9	9	610
1995-96	9	9	624
1996-97	18	13	1164
1997-98	51	42	4299
1998-99	64	50	5599
1999-00	69	55	6099

Source: Records of the union.

Other than the main dairy, union has 3 MCCs in the district: Gokak (20000 litres/day), Ramadurg (6000 litres/day), and Athani (4000 litres/day). MCC-wise distribution of WDCSs is given in Table 3.17 and they are equally spread over first three places. Athini is the northern most taluka of the district adjacent to Kolhapur (Maharashtra). There is a heavy competition for procurement in this area from both private and cooperative dairies of Maharashtra. As mentioned earlier the district has a marketable surplus of 2.64 lakh litres/day and the union is struggling to procure 1/5th (56000 litres/day) of this. Rest of the milk is collected by these dairies (12) who pay higher prices which is offset by higher selling prices in Bombay market. These dairies include Kolhapur milk union, Warana milk union, Mayur, Aarogya, Dampo, Mata, Yes, Yelgud, Krishna, Mahedils, Neppani, Ganeshwadi, Hutatma, Somaiah, etc.

Table 3.17

Chilling Centre-wise Distribution of All Women DCSs, 1999-00

Sl. No.	*MCC*	*Women DCSs*	*Membership*
1.	Main dairy	19	1993
2.	Gokak	17	1785
3.	Ramadurg	17	2125
4.	Athani	2	196
	Total	55	6099

Source: Records of the union.

Progress in procurement, sales, and production of cream, ghee, and peda is presented in Table 3.18. Procurement increased from 58.31 lakh litres in 1985-86 to 205.79 lakh litres in 1999-00. Reasons for enhanced milk procurement during 1992-93 and 1993-94 are already explained in previous paragraphs. Procurement was again picked up in 1999-00. The milk so procured is sold as fluid milk of different grades (tonned, double tonned, and standardised) in all taluka headquarters of the district. Sale of fluid milk too increased from 32.81 lakh litres in 1985-86 to 167.30 lakh litres in 1999-00. On an average, the union is marketing 45836 literes/day and 1/2 of it is sold in Goa. The union is not in a position to market its milk in the district due to stiff competition from a host of private dairies. Added to it, their timings, low commission to agents, absence of aggressive marketing, etc. also contributing to the problems. As a matter of fact, the union is struggling hard to increase its share in the market, but no results. In order to utilise sales volumes, the union purposes to: (a) create a separate department of marketing, (b) provide incentives to salesmen and commission agents, (c) arrange schemes to attract consumers through parlours, (d) assure availability of milk between 5.00 am to 10.00 pm. and (e) educate consumers about quality milk and soliciting consumers opinion about their milk.

Table 3.18

Progress in Procurement and Sales, 1986-00

Year	*Procurement (lakh litres)*	*Sale of fluid milk (lakhs litres)*	*Products manufactured*		
			cream (tonnes)	*Peda (tonnes)*	*Ghee (tonnes)*
1985-86	58.31	32.81	0	0	0
1986-87	94.37	71.87	0	0	0
1987-88	97.96	54.31	0	0	0
1988-89	84.62	63.47	188	8,118	217.5
1989-90	90.26	77.91	0,202	6,185	Nil
1990-91	116.91	80.89	0,388	0,852	95
1991-92	131.72	107.63	0,440	3,381	17,582
1992-93	195.79	124.30	1,567	5,456	34,640
1993-94	185.62	155.22	94,357	6,921	35,123
1994-95	152.76	151.42	29,758	4,931	12,588
1995-96	138.31	157.19	139,056	4,550	49,403
1996-97	169.03	178.19	155,845	4,650	76,208
1997-98	184.60	144.14	200,320	7,116	75,175
1998-99	184.46	144.95	35,699	5,424	22,277
1999-00	205.79	167.30	75,132	6,243	32,374

Source: Records of the union.

Apart from selling liquid milk, the union has been manufacturing cream, ghee, and peda whose progress is shown in Table 3.18. Off late, it started converting excess milk into skim milk powder through a private dairy.

Table 3.19

Progress in Sales and Net Profit (Rs. lakhs), 1986-00

Year	*Sales*	*Net profit/loss*
1985-86	21.94	+ 7.84
1986-87	14.13	-11.67
1987-88	27.26	-14.52
1988-89	405.61	+ 0.39
1989-90	708.68	-10.18
1990-91	740.31	-27.13
1991-92	917.39	+5.15
1992-93	2394.41	-110.85
1993-94	1823.77	-185.77
1994-95	1554.23	-130.13
1995-96	1771.23	-3.69
1996-97	2356.31	+34.49
1997-98	2277.86	+69.34
1998-99	2634.15	-37.11
1999-00	2904.97	-91.24

Source: Records of the union.

The union's sales increased from Rs. 21.94 lakhs to Rs. 2904.97 lakhs during the study period (Table 3.19). It posted net losses during 10 out of 15 years of the study period. Some of the reasons for heavy losses during 1993-96 are explained earlier. Further, hike in employees salaries from 1996, enhanced diesel and electricity price too contributed to heavy losses. Due to inadequate water supply of its own, the union is paying Rs. 60,000/ month towards water charges. The interest payable to NDDB/year is around Rs. 60.00 lakhs. Appointment of additional veterinarians, and temporary workers too contributed their might in this.

Table 3.20

Progress in Input Services Provided, 1986-00

Year	*Cattle feed (tonnes)*	*Fodder demo plots*	*AIs done*	*Calves born*	*Cases treated*
1985-86	583	187	7113	795	22913
1986-87	675	373	13733	2588	8129
1987-88	906	645	17773	3492	15805
1988-89	1132	1027	19698	3787	17412
1989-90	1317	1156	21383	4589	18491
1990-91	1882	1185	25354	5640	19420
1991-92	2293	1866	31544	6500	24436
1992-93	3959	1033	39829	8750	33018
1993-94	3163	2522	44354	10243	5693
1994-95	2852	3280	46321	13275	8025
1995-96	2638	2850	37263	11433	10256
1996-97	2354	1433	33322	8922	8078
1997-98	2460	2401	37260	10300	14791
1998-99	3576	1993	43950	12182	21581
1999-00	4463	3515	48761	13269	22494

Source: Records of the union.

As mentioned earlier, one of the objectives of the union has been provision of inputs to producer members at no loss no profit basis. In this regard union has been supplying balanced cattle feed, organising fodder demonstration plots by distributing mini kits, extending artificial insemination services, and health care (vaccination, veterinary camps, and emergency treatment). Progress in these activities is presented in Table 3.20. Though the cattle feed supply increased over time, it is less as a proportion of milk procured (0.500 kg. of cattle feed for every kg. of milk procured). It is to be mentioned here that local farmers feed brawn, husks of grams, maize and bajra seeds which leads to high cost of production without their knowledge (they are home grown!). Feeding of balanced cattle feed consisting of carbohydrates, proteins, vitamins, and minerals should be popularised. Vitamin A is very rich in green fodders which is in turn important for regular heat in animals. Balanced green fodder ration should be in the proportion of 0.75:0.25 of non-leguminous and leguminous crops.

Dry fodders have legnin content which is not easily digested by ruminents. Modern techniques like treating straw with urea, chauffing into small pieces, and treating with salt, urea, and jaggery will go a long way in proper utilisation of these materials. Promoting fodder plots thus help in reducing cost of production. However, there is no consistency in their growth. It mostly depended on the money made available for this purpose (more the allotment more plots and vice versa!).

Table 3.21

Viability of Functional Societies, 1986-00

Year	*Functional DCSs*	*Procurement/ society/day (litres)*	*Amount paid to producers (Rs. lakhs)*	*DCSs in profit*	*DCSs in loss*
1985-86	84	190	N.A.	75	9
1986-87	123	210	N.A.	113	10
1987-88	137	196	N.A.	120	7
1988-89	189	123	350.91	177	12
1989-90	204	121	250.94	193	11
1990-91	237	135	517.79	223	14
1991-92	268	135	656.15	258	10
1992-93	307	175	1221.64	207	10
1993-94	314	162	1187.34	307	7
1994-95	307	136	901.23	293	11
1995-96	292	130	953.87	280	12
1996-97	298	155	1510.65	284	14
1997-98	333	152	1609.87	327	6
1998-99	335	151	1413.18	319	16
1999-00	342	165	1811.48	330	12

Source: Records of the union.

The union has 12 veterinarians (7 on consolidated basis) attending 400 cases/month. On an average a veterinarian visits a DCS once in 3 months. In addition to union veterinarians, Department of Animal Husbandry, Government of Karnataka has its own network in the district. They too attend similar cases. AIs performed increased from 7113 in 1985-86 to 48761 in 1999-00 while calves born from 795 to 13269 during the same period (27%). AIs are also performed by the trained secretaries/ testers of the DCSs. Union has been supplying LN2 container, semen straws, and trevis and farmer is charged Rs. 10/AI (earlier it was provided free of cost). Of this, the secretary/ tester gets Rs. 5 as honorarium.

Table 3.22

Status of Employees, 2000

Section	*Managers*	*Super-visors*	*Techni-cians*	*Clerks*	*Drivers*	*Workers*	*Total*
Procurement and inputs	14	23	0	2	0	0	39
Production	1	4	0	0	0	10	15
Engineering	1	0	11	0	8	7	27
Quality control	0	1	0	0	0	8	9
Purchase and Stores	0	1	0	3	0	1	5
MIS	0	0	0	1	0	0	1
Marketing	2	1	0	0	0	18	21
Finance and Accounts	2	2	0	7	0	2	13
Administration	0	1	0	0	0	2	3
Chilling centres	0	3	2	0	0	4	9
Others	0	1	0	0	0	1	2
Canteen	0	0	0	1	0	0	1
Total	20	37	13	14	8	53	145

Source: Records of the union.

An attempt is made in Table 3.21 to analyse the performance of functional societies in terms of procurement, DCSs in profit/loss, and amount paid to producers/annum. Functional societies increased from 84 to 342 during the study period (1/3rd of the registered DCSs are defunct, refer Table 3.15). There is no consistency in procurement/DCS/day. Initially, it was around 200 litres/day, declined substantially during 1989-92, picked up during the next two years and later declined again. Currently, it is hovering around 160 litres/day/DCS. These DCSs collects milk twice daily, and make payments either once a week, or thrice a month or fortnightly depending on the decision of a particular DCS. However, union deposits the amount in the account of the DCS once a week on the 10th day.

It is to be mentioned here that the payments by the union is irregular for the last two years. At the time of investigation (January-February, 2001), payment was kept pending 40 days. It happened during 1993-95 too. Discussion with the producer members revealed that regular payment is the precondition to have faith/loyalty to the union. Members are not keen about input services as such facilities readily available in the village/ nearby. They are insisting on enhanced rates for milk and regular payment. Competitors are paying at the moment, a rupee/litre of milk extra and on regular basis. Their collection centres are well equipped with modern equipment and aesthetic. Their timings too are more convenient than DCSs. Further, private dairies are providing loans for purchasing animals, supply of feed, and health care facilities. They follow practical approach by contacting the opposition party or key person in the community/village and thus create a division among members and succeed in getting a large chunk of milk. Cooperatives over a period of 15-18 years worked for the development/promotion of dairying in this part of the country, they taught villagers about cattle management, clean milk production, marketing, etc. Spearhead team members worked for 15-16 hours/day in these villages and helped organising dairy cooperatives. But all of a sudden, due to liberalisation, a mushrooming of dairies had come up and are enjoying the benefits without any efforts. Whom to blame for this situation?

What ever may be the reason, union has to improve efficiency by reducing overhead expenses, leakages, improve marketing network and pay a reasonable price so as to bring back producers loyalty. If necessary, few uneconomical routes may be closed. NDDB may be approached for some soft loan/ freezing their interest burden. Unfortunately, the union's hands are tight in a way. Both producers prices and consumers prices are fixed by KMF and any small change in pricing would require lengthy time. The state government too would be unhappy to increase consumers price. Thus, on both the ends, it is helpless. The elected management should exercise its authority, take active interest, and see that things are put on right direction.

Table 3.21 also provides amounts paid to producers/ annum. Union paid as much as Rs. 18.11 crores in 1999-00, a big sum indeed for rural development. Baring few (12 in 1999-00) DCSs, majority of them are in profits and total profits of these DCSs are to the tune of Rs. 1.22 crores.

The union has in all 145 permanent employees (Table 3.22) and 60 daily wage workers. Procurement and inputs section employs as many as 39 followed by engineering (27).

Bangalore Urban and Rural District Cooperative Milk Producers Societies Union Limited (BAMUL)

Organised efforts to provide quality milk to urban consumers Bangalore were started in 1962 by establishing a 2000 litres/day MCC chilling centre at Byrapatna. It was followed by another MCC with a capacity of 10,000 litres/day at Anekal. These efforts were strengthened by establishing Bangalore dairy, a joint venture of UNICEF, Government of India, and Government of Karnataka in 1965. Another MCC was organised at Doddaballapura with 20,000 litres/day capacity. The Bangalore dairy had an initial capacity to process 50,000 litres/day which was increased to 1.50 lakh litres/day in 1975. The dairy, which was under the control of Government of Karnataka, was transferred to the Karnataka Dairy Development Corporation in 1975. Later, it was covered under Operation Flood Programme-II and III. Soon after, transfer of the dairy from Government of Karnataka to KDDC took place.

The dairy started organising dairy cooperative societies with the help of NDDB. Subsequently, Bangalore cooperative milk union limited was organised, covering Bangalore and and Kolar districts, in 1976. The union was bifurcated into (a) Bangalore urban and rural district cooperative milk producers societies union Limited, and (b) Kolar district cooperative milk producers societies union Limited, in 1987.

The installed capacity of Bangalore dairy was further expanded to 3.50 lakh litres/day in 1994 and 6 lakh litres/day in 2000. During this period, three more MCCs were started at the Jayapura (1995), Solur (1999), and Hosakota (2000). The union currently has 11 talukas with 2394 revenue villages. It has 4.48 lakh milch animals (1.62 lakh local milch cows, 1.96 lakh crossbred cows, and 0.90 lakh buffaloes) in its command area, 44% of the total milch animals are crossbreds. Total milk production in its jurisdiction is to the tune of 6.90 lakh litres/day of which 1.0 lakh litres/day is retained for home consumption. Thus, the marketable surplus is 5.90 lakh litres of which 4.97 litres/day is procured by the union, (84% of the total marketable surplus is procured by the union itself). Average fat in milk is 4.1% and SNF is 8.55% (for more details about the union, please see BAMUL, 2000).

Objectives of the Union

The union has following objectives:

(a) to provide assured and remunerative market for milk supplied by member producers,

(b) to supply good quality milk and milk products to urban consumers at competitive prices, and

(c) to organise dairy cooperative societies in villages and provide technical inputs to promote milk production and thus to facilitate rural development.

In the light of above objectives, an attempt is made in the following paragraphs to discuss the progress of the union.

Membership

Primary dairy cooperative societies (DCSs) are members of the union, and registered DCSs increased from 441 in 1985 to 1225 DCSs in 1999-00 while that of functional DCSs from 393 to 1165 during the same period (Table 3.23). Thus, the number of defunct societies stood at 60 in 1999-00. There were as many as 73046 producer members in 1985-86 and is increased to 2.18 lakhs by 1999-00. The union has 72 milk procurement rates connecting 1210 DCSs covering 13400 kms/day. Of the total membership as much as 15% are women. The increase in women membership is gradual over the study period. An analysis of figures on procurement of milk by these DCSs reveals interesting facts. There are as many as 770 DCSs procuring more than 300 litres/day in 1999-00. Further, 312 DCSs procured more than 500 litres/day in 1999-00. There are 221 DCSs procuring between 201-300 litres/day. Thus, as many as 921 DCSs, out of 1225 whose procurement is more than 200 litres/day in 1997-00. This shows the strengths of the union (Table 3.24). An interesting fact that can be noticed from Table 3.24 is that over the period the number of DCSs procuring less than 200 litres/day were pushed to higher brackets.

Performance of the DCSs is provided in Table 3.25. Performance is measured in terms of procurement/day, procurement price, DCSs in profits, and losses. Barring few years, average procurement/DCS increased during 1988-00 and currently it is 426 litres/day. There is steady increase in procurement price/litre which increased from Rs. 4.97/litre in 1987-88 to Rs. 8.78/litre in 1999-00. The number of loss making DCSs are few in number and net losses incurred by these DCSs is many times less than the profits posted by the majority of the DCSs. Special efforts may be initiated to achieve profits in all the DCSs in the union.

Table 3.23
Progress in Membership at Bangalore Milk Union, 1986-00

Year	*DCSs registered*	*DCSs functional*	*Men*	*Women*	*Total*
1985-86	441	393	63459	9581	73040
1986-87	530	479	70145	10590	80735
1987-88	535	510	87162	11349	98511
1988-89	645	606	99822	12377	112199
1989-90	671	644	107078	12976	120054
1990-91	721	676	117356	13829	131185
1991-92	737	723	119400	14875	134275
1992-93	785	763	128544	16309	144853
1993-94	846	803	136252	17154	153406
1994-95	929	852	151608	19429	171037
1995-96	964	918	163790	22899	186689
1996-97	1056	994	166775	25165	191940
1997-98	1117	1055	176848	29426	206274
1998-99	1173	1119	182279	31218	213497
1999-00	1225	1165	185166	32827	217993

Source: Records of the union.

Table 3.24
Procurement-wise Distribution of DCSs, 1995-00

Procurement (litre/day)	*1994-95*	*1995-96*	*1996-97*	*1997-98*	*1998-99*	*1999-00*
Less than 50	16	30	22	22	21	12
51-100	31	51	54	55	56	21
101-200	160	66	161	210	215	141
201-300	191	203	221	225	233	221
More than 300	454	468	536	543	594	770
Total	852	918	994	1055	1119	1165

Source: Records of the union.

Table 3.25

Performance of DCSs, 1988-00

Year	*Average/day Procurement/ DCS (litre/ day)*	*Average procurement price (Rs. liter)*	*DCSs under profit*	*Amount of profit (Rs. lakhs)*	*DCSs under loss*	*Amount of loss (Rs. lakhs)*
1987-88	367	4.50	4.97	142.29	13	1.82
1988-89	327	4.65	562	161.21	44	1.74
1989-90	347	4.85	625	150.29	19	1.80
1990-91	308	5.05	646	132.39	30	4.80
1991-92	275	5.88	684	188.50	39	3.85
1992-93	317	6.08	751	281.16	12	2.67
1993-94	364	6.52	771	302.13	32	4.17
1994-95	363	6.33	829	337.63	23	7.63
1995-96	383	6.96	896	428.85	22	7.83
1996-97	397	7.98	974	527.21	20	5.34
1997-98	384	8.35	1034	586.78	20	2.58
1998-99	379	8.68	1084	673.51	35	3.99
1999-00	426	8.78	1146	792.23	26	10.69

Source: Records of the union.

The union has three lady supervisors and a dedicated and energetic Deputy Manager exclusively to organise and develop of the WDCSs. They work as a team and all of them were trained at NDDB and IRMA. In gender sensitization, planning and management of WDCSs. Progress of WDCSs is provided in Table 3.26. The first WDCS was registered at Kotamaranahalli under Byrapatna MCC on August 30, 1991. It's current procurement is 546 litres/day. By the end of March 31, 2000, there were 58 WDCSs with a total membership of 9379. Of the 58 WDCSs, 52 were organised under STEP programme. MCC-wise distribution of WDCSs is given in Table 3.27. Byrapatna MCC has 18, while Hosakote and Solur each has 14 WDCSs.

Table 3.26

Progress in All Women DCSs, 1986-00

Year	*WDCSs*	*Membership*
1985-86	0	0
1986-87	0	0
1987-88	0	0
1988-89	0	0
1989-90	0	0
1990-91	0	0
1991-92	1	215
1992-93	1	215
1993-94	2	421
1994-95	3	683
1995-96	6	1321
1996-97	6	1321
1997-98	25	4034
1998-99	50	8481
1999-00	58	9379

Source: Records of the union.

MCC-wise and procurement-wise distribution of WDCSs is given in Table 3.28. There are only three WDCSs procuring less than 100 litres/day. (no WDCS below 50 litres/day). As may as 35 WDCSs have been procuring more than 200 litres/day. WDCSs like Cheemasandra (Hosakote MCC), Nayakanahally, Chakkere, and Kotamaranahally (Byrapatna MCC), Yelachagere (Solur MCC) procure more than 500 litres/day. KMF has drawn a scheme of incentive to WDCSs. Under the scheme a chair person/union from WDCSs procuring more than on an average 350 litres/day are eligible to participate in a competition. From among those competitors highest procuring WDCS would be selected as a champion WDCS and its chairperson is deputed to New Zealand and Australia for 10 days to get acquaintance with the latest developments in animal husbandry and dairying.

Table 3.27

MCC-wise Distribution of All Women DCSs, 1999-00

MCS	*WDCSs*	*Membership*
Hosakote	14	2152
Anekal	5	574
Doddaballapur	6	471
Vijayapura	1	75
Byrapatna	18	3690
Solur	14	2417
Total	58	9379

Source: Records of the union.

Table 3.28

MCC-wise Distribution of WDCSs with Range of Procurement

Procurement (litres/day)	*Hosakote*	*Anekal*	*Doddaballapur*	*Vijayapura*	*Byrapatna*	*Solur*	*Total*
<50	0	0	0	0	0	0	0
51-100	0	0	0	0	3	0	3
101-150	1	0	1	0	6	3	11
151-200	1	0	0	0	5	3	9
201-300	9	1	3	1	1	5	20
>300	3	4	2	0	3	3	15
Total	14	5	6	1	18	14	58

Source: Records of the union.

WDCSs were analysed across MCCs, and their age (Table 3.29). Only three WDCSs have completed more than five years of age and equal number have completed 4-5 years of working. Nine WDCSs have 3-4 years of existence. Most of them, 31, were having 2-3 years of working experience. As mentioned above about 50 WDCSs were organised since 1997-98 under STEP programme and same is apparent from Table 3.29.

Table 3.29

MCC-wise WDCSs on the Basis of Commissioning

Age of (years)	*Hosakote*	*Anekal*	*Doddaballa-pura*	*Vijaya-pura*	*Byra-patna*	*Solur*	*Total*
<1	0	1	1	0	0	0	2
1-2	2	2	1	0	2	3	10
2-3	10	2	3	1	9	6	31
3-4	1	0	1	0	3	4	9
4-5	1	0	0	0	2	0	3
>5	0	0	0	0	2	1	3
Total	14	5	6	1	18	14	58

Source: Records of the union.

Milk Procurement

The union has been experiencing an unprecedented rise in milk procurement. Average procurement/day steadily increased from 1.27 lakh litres in 1985-86 to 4.97 lakh litres in 1999-00, procurement increased at annual average growth rate of 25% (Table 3.30). The union could be able to procure and process milk due to commissioning and expansion of MCCs, installing additional pasteurizers, packaging machines, etc.

Raw and chilled milk received from MCCs through insulated tankers is pasteurized at the main dairy. Initially milk was marketed in bottles, but switched over to polythene sachets. Currently, the union is marketing milk and milk products in Bangalore city, Anekal, Kanakapura, and Sathnur thorugh 681 agents. Fluid milk sales increased from 2.48 lakh litres/day in 1987-88 to 4.32 lakh litres/day in 1999-00 (Table 3.30). The union is having a market share of about 35.40% in Bangalore city.

Table 3.30

Progress in Procurement and Sales, 1986-00

Year	*Procurement (lakh litres*	*Sale of luid milk*	*Butter (kgs/day)*	*Ghee (kgs/day)*	*Peda (kgs/day)*
1985-86	1.27	N.A.	N.A.	N.A.	N.A.
1986-87	1.62	N.A.	N.A.	N.A.	N.A.
1987-88	1.87	2.48	519	2821	50
1988-89	1.97	2.78	405	2751	67
1989-90	2.23	3.00	348	2199	125
1990-91	2.08	3.27	341	1792	205
1991-92	1.98	2.80	614	1282	199
1992-93	2.41	2.95	1580	1729	190
1993-94	2.92	3.12	2243	2164	192
1994-95	3.09	3.10	1095	2346	242
1995-96	3.52	3.10	2298	2009	209
1996-97	3.95	3.53	2766	1243	182
1997-98	4.05	3.87	1188	1407	193
1998-99	4.24	4.19	1911	1383	218
1999-00	4.97	4.32	2997	1550	228

Source: Records of the union.

Surplus milk is used to manufacture products like butter ghee, peda, curd, skim milk powder, flavoured milk, etc. (Table 3.30). Milk and milk products of the union are sold under the brand name of Nandini. Total turnover, net profit/loss, and reserve funds are provided in Table 3.31. Annual turnover in 1999-00 is Rs. 225.36 crores while it earned a net profit of Rs. 4.15 crores during the same year. It has more than six crore rupees as reserve fund.

Table 3.31
Progress in Total Turnover/Net Profits (Rs. lakhs), 1986-00

Year	*Turnover*	*Net profits*	*Reserve funds*
1985-86	103.82	-2.51	1.45
1986-87	162.36	-5.12	0.75
1987-88	122.69	-0.34	0.79
1988-89	4194.86	68.09	5.75
1989-90	7567.74	-12.65	79.75
1990-91	6924.22	-20.52	80.17
1991-92	7566.39	-84.08	100.31
1992-93	10371.38	-68.82	107.14
1993-94	10878.71	-5.45	108.01
1994-95	10282.29	84.13	69.14
1995-96	12257.97	270.43	232.48
1996-97	15438.88	383.76	253.14
1997-98	17125.33	497.62	273.74
1998-99	19776.20	674.93	300.47
1999-00	22536.33	414.89	622.75

Source: Records of the union.

The union is taking special care to promote health of members cattle. Veterinary facilities have been extended to all DCSs. Mobile veterinary routes, emergency veterinary routes, infertility camps, vaccination against foot and mouth disease, theileriasis, etc. are being regularly conducted. Progress in supply of technical inputs is provided in Table 3.32. There are (1999-00) 15 mobile veterinary routes (providing weekly free veterinary facilities) and 11 emergency routes to cater to animal health care. Together, 2.85 lakh animals were treated in 1999-00. Progress in AI centres, calves born, fodder plots organised is spectacular. Further, fodder seeds are being distributed to members at 50% subsidy. Technical advice on fodder cultivation too is provided. Chauff cutters are being supplied at 60% subsidy to ensure effective utilisation of fodder. Programmes were also taken up to conserve surplus fodder grown in rainy season and to use the same in lean season. Silage demonstration, treating paddy straw with urea, etc. were taken-up. The union procures balanced cattle feed from cattle feed plants of KMF for distribution among members (growth is shown in Table 3.32).

Table 3.32

Progress in Distribution of Technical Inputs, 1986-00

Year	*Mvr* *	*Emr* **	*Cases treated*		*AI centres*	*AIs done*	*Calves born*	*Fodder plots (acres)*	*Cattle feed (tonnes)*
			MVR	*Emr*					
1985-86	N.A.	N.A.	N.A.	N.A.	N.A.	N.A.	N.A.	N.A.	N.A.
1986-87	N.A.	N.A.	N.A.	N.A.	N.A.	N.A.	N.A.	N.A.	N.A.
1987-88	8	4	150430	25448	221	80402	13984	3484	5795
1988-89	9	5	127607	33615	260	95921	17590	2344	7206
1989-90	11	5	139278	25208	283	104387	20281	4775	9639
1990-91	10	5	137250	22214	300	108357	27509	5818	6389
1991-92	11	6	133678	22726	320	111642	31008	6536	5868
1992-93	12	7	192419	25483	331	117706	32112	3255	10028
1993-94	12	7	200562	26534	346	114437	32812	11135	12695
1994-95	12	7	187608	28395	302	116501	30731	4383	10968
1995-96	12	7	131856	27780	330	130188	39172	3552	8412
1996-97	15	7	165552	31152	358	136704	37606	8556	10416
1997-98	15	8	196872	32748	368	155988	38694	13560	10944
1998-99	15	9	221556	37368	386	178884	43880	14016	14136
1999-00	15	11	242556	42336	411	181908	47802	14568	18240

* Mvr: Mobile veterinary routes
** Emr: Emergency route
Source: Records of the union.

Table 3.33
Manpower Status

Section	*Managers*	*Officers/ Supervis-ors*	*Techni-cians*	*Supt./ Stenos/ clerks*	*Drivers*	*Workers*	*Total*
Procurement	20	76	0	17	4	16	133
Inputs	45	0	0	17	3	35	100
Production	8	9	0	16	0	222	255
Engineering	8	22	83	6	39	59	217
QualityControl	2	8	0	1	0	17	28
Purchase and stores	2	2	0	21	0	11	36
MIS	1	0	0	2	0	0	3
Marketing	3	3	0	17	0	90	113
Finance and accounts	2	4	0	63	0	15	84
Administration	0	2	0	19	0	8	29
MCCs	4	15	14	9	0	69	111
Time office	0	1	0	7	0	6	14
Canteen	1	0	0	5	0	13	19
LWO/PRO/ Telephone	1	1	0	6	0	7	15
MO/Health/ Garden	0	1	0	0	0	30	31
Security	0	3	0	3	0	33	39
Total	97	147	97	209	46	631	1227

Source: Records of the union.

The union has 1227 employees on its rolls (Table 3.33). Production department has 255 employees followed by procurement and inputs (233 employees), and engineering 217. The union is in the process of checking out a VRS and redeployment of manpower employees in a phase manner. The union got Best Productivity award in 1998-99 by National Productivity Council.

Table 3.34

Status of Selected Milk Unions of KMF, 1998-99

Indicator	*Bangalore*	*Belgaum*	*Raichur*	*State*
Geographical area (00 sq. kms)	80	134	224	1922
Population (000)	6512	3584	3966	44977
Bovine population (000)	771	1164	1445	14140
Crossbred animals (000)	219	52	30	1016
Union formed	1975	1983	1985	N.A
DCSs	1173	484	421	8235
Membership (lakhs)	1.82	0.74	0.49	15.22
Average procurement/ day (lakh kgs)	4.24	0.51	0.39	15.77
Average sales/day (lakh litres)	8.15	0.40	0.33	13.88

Source: Same as Table 3.1zs.

Comparison of Selected Milk Unions

As described above, Bangalore, Belgaum, and Raichur-Bellary milk unions are selected for the study. Area of operation as also bovine population of Bangalore milk union is lowest compared to Raichur and Belgaum. Bangalore is the oldest union while Raichur was formed in 1985. Other indicators considered (DCSs organised, membership, average procurement, and average sales) are the highest in Bangalore while it is the lowest in Raichur milk union (Table. 3.34).

Summary

Karnataka has a written history of more than 2000 years. It was formed in 1956 and renamed as Karnataka in 1973. Rice is the main food crop followed by maize, millets, and pulses. Scientific animal breeding was followed for the last 300 years in the state. Dairying in the state is one of the major activities which contributes substantially to the rural economy. Formal efforts for dairy development were started in 1974. Later KDDC was setup and finally KMF was organised in 1984. There are 13 milk unions covering 27 districts and as many as 8299 DCSs with 3.28 lakh pourer membership. Average procurement of milk touched a peak of 17.79 lakh litres/day as against a fluid milk sale of 14.42 lakh litres/day. A number of milk products too are being manufactured and sold under the brand name of Nandini. The federation's turnover is about Rs. 870 crores. With a view to involve women in dairy activities and to empower women of weak sections, STEP programme is being implemented in all 13 milk unions with the help of Ministry of Human Resources Development, Government of India. The programme is in its second phase (2001-03) now and the results so far have been impressive.

Raichur-Bellary milk union was registered in 1989. The area of operation of the milk union consists of 16 talukas from Bellary, Koppal, and Raichur districts. It has 386 functional DCSs with 42000 membership. Women constituted 28% of the total membership and there are 44 WDCSs in the milkshed. Milk procurement of the union increased from 109.34 lakh litres/annum in 1990-91 to 139.59 lakh litres/annum in 1999-00 and turnover stood at Rs. 17.17 crores.

Belgaum district cooperative milk union was registered in 1985. There are 504 DCSs with 56827 members, 69 WDCSs with 6099 members. Procurement of the union increased from 58.31 lakh litres in 1985-86 to 205.79 lakh litres in 1999-00, that of sale of fluid milk from 32.81 lakh litres to 167.30 lakh litres during the same period. Half of its milk is sold in Goa. Apart from manufacturing several grades of milk, products like cream, ghee, and peda are prepared here. Turnover of the union is Rs. 29.05 crores in 1999-00. The union has been supplying a number of technical inputs to producer members. There is stiff competition from a number of private dairies and the union's health is not satisfactory.

BAMUL has history of almost 40 years. Over a period of time it is evolved as one of the biggest and best milk unions of southern India. The area of the union comprises of Bangalore urban district (3 talukas) and Bangalore rural district (8 talukas) with a total of 2394 revenue villages. Currently it has 1225 DCSs of which 55 are WDCSs and 72 milk procurement routes with 1.82 lakh members. Its current installed capacity is 10 lakh litres/day. Average procurement/DCS is 431 litres/day and the union is paying Rs. 8.82/litre of cow milk. Average procurement is 4.97 lakh litres/ day (1999-00) and 87% of it is sold as fluid milk. The union has been providing a number of production enhancement inputs to milk producers. They include veterinary health care facilities, cattlefeed, artificial inseminations, fodder seeds, guidance, etc. The union got best productivity award in 1998-99 by National Productivity Council for its excellent performance.

Chapter 4

Performance of STEP and NON-STEP WDCSs

This chapter is devoted to analyse performance of 'all women dairy cooperative societies' (WDCSs) in different agro-climatic regions covered under STEP and NON-STEP. Both primary and secondary data are used, and averages for 1997-98 to 1999-2000 are presented in the following sections.

Performance of Selected WDCSs

The concept of 'all women dairy cooperative societies' (WDCSs) is very old and the first WDCS was organised in Kaira district of Gujarat in 1968. Since then, a number of other milk unions have also promoted the concept. Apart from the individual efforts of the milk unions, these WDCSs were also promoted with the help of international donor agencies and non-governmental organisations (NGOs). General impression about the working of the WDCSs has been that they are superior to mixed gender societies [Sen and Rani (1990), Rao (1995), Rao (1996), Rao (2000), and Rao (2001)]. Reasons quoted for their success include procurement of larger quantities of milk, economies in management, prudent financial management, group work, coordination, prior knowledge about the enterprise, etc. In the light of about literature, an attempt is made here to evaluate the performance of WDCSs in Andhra Pradesh and Karnataka.

Table 4.1

Performance of STEP and NON-STEP WDCSs, 1998-00

Indicator	*Andhra Pradesh*			*Karnataka*		
	STEP	*NON-STEP*	*Average*	*STEP*	*NON-STEP*	*Average*
1. Membership	53	95	75	85	65	75
2. Milk collection (litres/year)	34821	27740	31281	107036	42905	74975
3. Milk supplied/ member (litres/year)	657	292	478	1259	660	962
4. Value of milk (Rs./member)	5585	2515	4050	10702	5610	8156
5. Net profit (Rs.lakhs/year)	0.21	0.08	0.14	0.49	0.26	0.39
6. Cost of milk procurement (Rs./litre)	0.40	0.65	0.54	0.29	0.38	0.33

Source: Records of the selected WDCSs.

As mentioned earlier, performance of the WDCSs is measured in terms of membership, milk collection, amount paid to producers, other inputs supply, participation of management committee in the day to day of working of the WDCSs, contribution of employees, etc. Data on these parameters were collected separately for STEP and NON-STEP WDCSs and are provided in Table 4.1.

A close perusal of Table 4.1 reveals interesting results. The average membership/WDCS is same in the both states at the aggregated level. Within the states, membership is more in NON-STEP WDCSs of Andhra Pradesh while it is more in STEP WDCSs of Karnataka. As discussed earlier, STEP is three years old programme in the study area. While NON-STEP

WDCSs were formed as earlier as in 1980. Thus, NON-STEP WDCSs have been working for a longer time, rather they are stabilized by now. Some of them were started by giving financial assistance to members, in some cases no such assistance was given. Training was an integral part of some WDCSs organised under NON-STEP while others had no such advantage even. Thus, the WDCSs of NON-STEP are of heterogeneous features. As against this, WDCSs under STEP were organised by providing financial assistance wherein extensive training is a compulsory input. Training is provided to members, committee members, employees and training inputs included management of dairy cooperative society, financial management, animal healthcare, animal nutrition, legal literacy, health, adult education, nutrition, sanitation, etc. Further, as these societies are only three years old, mostly they are organised in small villages/hamlets where people belong to, nevertheless, small community having cohesiveness and homogeneous characters. In majority of the cases, they were formed on the basis of request and felt need of the women than requirement of the dairy officials. Thus, there is clear demarcation between the physical settings of these two WDCSs. These differences should be kept in mind while comparing two sets of WDCSs.

As of Andhra Pradesh, Chittoor is dominated by crossbred milk while Warangal and Prakasam, are served by buffalo milk. A comparison of STEP and NON-STEP WDCSs of Andhra Pradesh reveal that the performance of STEP WDCSs is better than NON-STEP WDCSs. Though NON-STEP WDCSs have more membership, their total milk collection/year, milk supplies/member/year, and net profits earned/year is low. As a result, cost of milk procurement is more in NON-STEP WDCSs. On the contrary, value of milk poured/member/year is 222% more in STEP WDCSs. This disparity is partly due to maintenance of crossbred cows by members of STEP WDCSs. The other factors are discussed in rest of this chapter.

The phenomenon is, nevertheless, same in Karnataka too. Bangalore is endowed by 100% cow milk while Belgaum, and Bellary, it is again mixed milk shared equally among cows and buffaloes. STEP WDCSs again maintained their superiority over their counterparts in the state. An examination of performance of WDCSs in Andhra Pradesh and Karnataka reveal that WDCSs in Karnataka, on an average, did well over their counterparts in Andhra Pradesh. Figures presented in Chapters 2 and 3 too provided such inferences. Milk collection/ WDCS/year is 2.4 times more in Karnataka which resulted is higher payments to members and reduced cost of milk procurement. Cost of milk procurement/litre of is just 33 paise in Karnataka while it is 54 paise in Andhra Pradesh.

Table 4.2

Progress in Input Supplies through STEP and NON-STEP WDCSs, 1998-00

Indicator	*Andhra Pradesh*			*Karnataka*		
	STEP	*NON-STEP*	*Average*	*STEP*	*NON-STEP*	*Average*
1. Cattle feed (bags of 70 kgs)	100	48	74	525	128	327
2. Fodder seeds (kgs)	35	15	25	105	46	76
3. AIs done	180	100	140	350	215	283
4. Calves born	54	25	41	133	65	99
5. Members trained (%)	25	02	13	43	14	28
6. Committee members Trained (%)	85	32	59	100	45	71
7. Secretary training (%)	100	40	70	100	58	79

Source: Records of the selected WDCSs.

WDCSs under study are based on 'Anand Pattern' wherein primaries (WDCSs) are the grassroot level organisations, they are federated into a district milk union, and a group of such milk unions form a state level federation. Major function of the primaries is to provide a remunerative price to the milk produced by its members, round the year. Apart from providing regular market, these primaries also provide a number of production enhancement inputs like balanced cattle feed, fodder seeds/saplings, artificial insemination facilities, health care, training to members/employees, contributions to village amenities, etc. Data on some of these facilities provided by WDCSs are given in Table 4.2.

STEP WDCSs once again registered their superiority by delivering more facilities to its member producers. For example, STEP WDCSs of Andhra Pradesh supplied as much as 7,000 kgs of cattle feed/year as against 3360 kgs by NON-STEP WDCSs/year. In other words, STEP WDCSs sold 0.201 kgs of feed/litre of milk procured while NON-STEP WDCSs supplied 0.121 kgs of feed/litre of milk collected. Recommended level of cattle feed/litre of milk is 0.500 kgs. However, this scientific standard depends on the availability and quantum green fodder, intake of dry fodders, milk production, and body weight of the animal. On the whole, WDCSs of Andhra Pradesh supplied less than the desired level of cattle feed to its members. This could be one reason for low milk yields in the area. According to respondents, less intake of feed is also due to its high cost. As regards Karnataka, WDCSs of STEP sold as much as 36750 kgs of cattle feed/year while NON-STEP WDCSs sold 8960 kgs/year. Thus, the NON-STEP WDCSs supplied the lowest (0.209 kgs/litre of milk procured) while STEP WDCSs supplied 0.343 kgs/litre of milk procured. A comparison of WDCSs of Andhra Pradesh and Karnataka revealed that WDCSs of Karnataka performed better than their counterparts in Andhra Pradesh. Similar pattern is noticed in other parameters considered. Interestingly, all secretaries of STEP WDCSs from both the states were trained.

Table 4.3

Socio-economic Status of Committee Members

Particulars	*Andhra Pradesh*			*Karnataka*		
	STEP (N=108)	*NON- (N=108)*	*Average (n=216)*	*STEP (N=108)*	*NON- (N=108)*	*AVERAGE (n=216)*
Age	32.3	45.6	40.5	30.4	35.8	32.8
Education						
Illiterate (%)	13.9	22.2	18.0	10.2	20.4	15.3
can sign (%)	19.4	18.5	19.0	22.2	26.9	24.5
less than 5 (%)	31.5	36.2	33.8	26.9	19.4	23.1
6-10 (%)	18.5	12.0	15.3	22.2	23.1	22.7
11 and (%) above (%)	16.7	11.1	13.9	18.5	10.2	14.4
Caste						
FC (%)	51.9	55.6	53.7	23.1	59.3	41.2
BC (%)	31.5	33.3	32.4	63.0	17.6	40.3
SC/ST (%)	16.6	11.1	13.9	13.9	23.1	18.5
Land holding (ha)						
landless (%)	11.1	9.3	10.2	13.0	14.8	13.9
0.1-1.0 (%)	18.5	23.2	20.8	16.7	22.2	19.5
1.1-2.0 (%)	24.0	21.3	22.7	20.4	16.7	18.5
2.1-4.0 (%)	28.8	22.2	25.5	33.3	20.4	26.8
4.1 and above (%)	17.6	24.0	20.8	16.6	25.9	21.3
Number of years on committee	3.0	5.5	4.2	3.0	6.0	4.8

Source: Field study.

Further, quantity of sour/low quality/curdled milk is more in NON-STEP WDCSs compared to STEP WDCSs which reflects of the quality of milk and members awareness about such losses among STEP WDCSs. Apart from above variations in quantitative variables, an attempt is also made to focus attention on socio-economic status of committee members.

WDCSs are managed by a nine member elected committee whose term is three years. Thus, in all 108 committee members represented STEP WDCSs and equal number in NON-STEP WDCSs of Andhra Pradesh. Same is true with Karnataka also. This analysis is carried out mainly because it is ultimately the management which is responsible for the health of an organisation. An enlightened, dedicated, and visionary management is proactive and responsible to new ideas, and committed to development of the organisation/members.

A close observation of Table 4.3 indicate that average age of committee members across board is around 40 which is a good sign. However, there are variations across categories. The average age of committee members among STEP WDCSs, irrespective of the state, is less than that of NON-STEP WDCSs and interestingly it is once again less in Karnataka compared to Andhra Pradesh. This indicate that relatively young and energetic women are participating in the management of WDCSs in Karnataka than in Andhra Pradesh.

Educational status of these committee members reveals interesting results. About 67% of women of STEP WDCSs from Andhra Pradesh have formal education. As many as 16.7% have studied up to 11th standard or more while it is 11.1% in NON-STEP WDCSs. Thus, 33% of women in STEP WDCSs and 41% of women in NON-STEP WDCSs are illiterate, thereby indicating relatively high proportion illiterates in NON-STEP WDCSs. More or less similar results are obtained for WDCSs of Karnataka. Thus, it may be concluded that majority of the WDCSs members of WDCSs in the study area are literate. Apart from formal literacy, there is a category of women who 'can sign'. These are the enterprising women who have been attending adult education classes in their leisure times and trying to learn. Some of the respondents made it through sons/daughters and are proud to sign at this age. There are some women who are members of self-help group wherein such training classes are being conducted. Thus, there is a movement/campaign through WDCSs or state government or NGOs to make women literate and the results are evident from Table 4.3.

Caste-wise, and land holding-wise analysis of the committee members indicate clear domination of these prestigious posts by dominant castes with higher land holdings. With exception in STEP WDCSs of Karnataka. Most of the committee members are continuing for several years by getting reelected/re-nominated to the positions. Thus, literate members of high castes with larger land holdings have, nevertheless, cornered the positions of committee members of the WDCSs in the study areas. Mostly these members have a strong base in the village through their husbands/in-laws. Representation of SCs/STs is nominal and for name sake. A large number of committee meetings attended by the author brought out the fact that there is clear demarcation and treatments to different caste members in these meetings. In general, members belonging to lower castes sit in the last rows preferably on floor and hardly participate in decision making process. They are also the last people to take refreshment and first to leave the meetings.

Table 4.4

Issues Discussed in Committee Meetings

Issue	*Andhra Pradesh*			*Karnataka*		
	STEP (n=108)	*Non-step*	*Average (n=216) (n=108)*	*STEP (n=108)*	*Non-step (n=108)*	*Average (n=216*
Meetings/year	6.3	3.5	4.9	9.5	4.0	7.0
Attendance in committee meetings (%)	57.5	40.3	48.9	83.3	54.0	65.6
Profit/loss	64	35	99	86	45	131
Increasing procurement	35	27	62	75	56	131
Enrolling members	30	15	45	77	32	109
Salaries to employees	55	32	87	80	45	125

(Contd.)

Issue	*Andhra Pradesh*			*Karnataka*		
	STEP (n=108)	*Non-step*	*Average (n=216) (n=108)*	*STEP (n=108)*	*Non-step (n=108)*	*Average (n=216*
Guarantee to members for purchase of animals	45	23	68	74	37	111
Deputing members to training	60	15	75	77	28	105
Complaints about fat testing	35	22	57	65	41	106
Milk/fat losses during transit	47	31	78	57	42	99
Supply of other inputs	28	18	46	35	20	55

As members gave multiple answers totals are more than sample size.

Source: Field study.

Committee meetings are organised every month to monitor progress and take precautionary measures for successful working of the WDCSs. Agenda is circulated by the secretary (paid employee) a week's advance and signatures obtained. These meetings are generally conducted in the premises of the WDCSs and mostly women attend these meetings. It has been noticed that meetings are very regular in STEP WDCSs of Karnataka followed by their counterparts in Andhra Pradesh. However, they were not conducted on regular basis in NON-STEP WDCSs (Table 4.4). It is, once again, to be mentioned here that STEP WDCSs are little more than three years old and got substantial financial and training inputs which made them aware of the functioning of WDCSs and economies of dairy farming. They are being, so far, monitored regularly by the staff of milk union who provides necessary guidance/help. This made them to be alert and regular while it is not so in NON-STEP WDCSs.

As expected, STEP WDCSs again had higher number of meetings/year than NON-STEP WDCSs in both states. They recorded higher turnouts too in those meetings. As much as 83.3% of the members were present in such meetings in Karnataka while attendance is the lowest (40%) in NON-STEP WDCSs of Andhra Pradesh. Low levels of awareness, lack of monitory benefits, low procurement, interference by well to do, etc. could be reasons for this low attendance.

Committee members were asked to mention issues discussed in these meetings on priority and they are presented in Table 4.4. Discussion on 'profit/loss for the period or month' is the single important factor which majority of the members mentioned. This is followed by efforts to increase procurement, enrolling new members, salaries to employees, guarantee to members for purchase of milch animals, deputing members to training, complaints about irregular fat testing, milk and/or fat losses during transit, and supply of others inputs are the other issues discussed in committee members in that order. Sending members to training is rarely noticed in NON-STEP WDCSs while it is a very frequent phenomenon in STEP WDCSs.

A word about fat testing is in order here. As per the 'Anand Pattern' milk is paid in the basis of its quality (fat and SNF), thus twice daily testing is a must. Testers are trained by the union for a week on both gerber test and milko-tester. In about 35% of the STEP WDCSs, testing is not adhered to and more so in NON-STEP WDCSs (70%). Testing is done twice or three a month and payment is made on this basis. Wherever WDCSs received substandard quality report from the union, the WDCS maintained vigil and culprits are caught. Testing is avoided because of the negligence of the secretary/tester, ignorance of the members, lack of chemicals, etc. There are instances that such defects were encashed by few elite members which led to clashes/differences among members. It is in the interest of the WDCSs that testing is done regularly to maintain discipline among its members.

General body is the highest decision making authority of a WDCS, while management committee works for the implementation of the decisions taken in the general body. Paid employees attend day to work (collection, payment, maintenance of records, organising meetings, arranging input supplies, etc). Depending up on the quantum of procurement, employees (secretary, accountant, tester, and helper) are paid at a WDCS. Secretary is like a chief executive officer and yields considerable influence in the village and WDCS. WDCSs have women employees in many places and more so in the case of STEP societies. It is aimed at involving women in managing WDCS and also providing employment and income for rural women. However, out of 24 WDCSs, 8 have women secretaries in Andhra Pradesh and 16 have women in Karnataka. Women members felt comfortable with same sex than men. This helped them in sharing their grievances, difficulties, and happiness.

Table 4.5

Particulars of Paid Employees, 1999-00

Particulars	*Andhra Pradesh*			*Karnataka*		
	STEP	*NON-STEP*	*Average*	*STEP*	*NON-STEP*	*Average*
Number of employees/WDCS	1.33	2.17	1.75	2.83	2.50	2.67
Age	29.5	41.0	35.3	25.3	39.4	32.4
Educational qualification						
illiterate	3 (18.8)	2 (8.7)	5 (12.8)	0 (0.0)	1 (3.3)	1 (1.5)
1-5	1 (6.1)	1 (4.3)	2 (5.1)	5 (14.7)	4 (13.3)	9 (14.1)
6-10	5 (31.3)	12 (52.2)	17 (43.6)	15 (44.1)	13 (43.3)	28 (43.8)
11 and above	7 (43.8)	8 (34.8)	15 (38.5)	14 (41.2)	12 (40.0)	26 (40.6)
Total	16 (100.0)	23 (100.0)	39 (100.0)	34 (100.0)	30 (100.0)	64 (100.0)

(Contd.)

Particulars	*Andhra Pradesh*			*Karnataka*		
	STEP	*NON-STEP*	*Average*	*STEP*	*NON-STEP*	*Average*
Caste						
(a) Secretary						
FC	9 (75.0)	7 (58.3)	16 (66.7)	10 (83.3)	8 (66.7)	18 (75.0)
BC	3 (25.0)	5 (41.7)	8 (33.3)	2 (16.7)	4 (33.3)	6 (25.0)
SC/ST	0 (0.0)	0 (0.0)	0 (0.0)	0 (0.0)	0 (0.0)	0 (0.0)
Total	12 (100.0)	12 (100.0)	24 (100.0)	12 (100.0)	12 (100.0)	24 (100.0)
b) Other employees						
FC	2 (50.0)	3 (27.3)	5 (33.3)	7 (31.8)	8 (44.4)	15 (37.5)
BC	2 (50.0)	5 (45.4)	7 (46.7)	10 (45.5)	4 (22.3)	14 (35.0)
SC/ST	0 (0.0)	3 (27.3)	3(20.0)	5(22.7)	6(33.3)	11(27.5)
Total	4 (100.0)	11 (100.0)	15 (100.0)	22 (100.0)	18 (100.0)	40 (100.0)
Salary bill (Rs./month)	13600	21275	17438	34000	24000	29000
Time spent/ employee (hours/day)	4.3	3.5	3.9	6.2	5.1	5.6
Average milk procurement/ employee (litres/year)	2176	1206	1691	3148	1430	2289

Source: Field study.

Average number of employees/WDCS is the highest (2.83) in STEP WDCSs of Karnataka while rest ranged between 1.33 to 2.50 (Table 4.5). As regards age of the secretaries, STEP WDCSs have relatively younger people and about 40% them, in both the states, studied more than 10th class. This indicates that young and educated youth are looking after WDCSs in the study area. The post of secretary (a key post in the WDCS) is again cornered (67-75%) by people belonging to upper castes while in few cases (when there is no competition) it is occupied by BCs. Quite sadly, no SC/ST candidate is allowed to hold this portfolio. Facts pertaining to distribution of other employees too revealed same picture. However, a few such unimportant posts were distributed among SCs/STs. This reveals that though WDCSs created employment opportunities for rural people, they are usurped by rich and dominant caste people.

Table 4.6

Difference in Members' Perceptions Regarding Quality of Services Extended sby WDCSs of Andhra Pradesh

Service and its quality	*STEP (n=60)*	*NON-STEP (n=60)*	*Absolute 'Z' value*
Milk collection			
(a) Regular	43	40	0.8545
(b) Not very regular	10	12	0.6789
(c) Very irregular	2	2	0.0000
(d) No opinion	5	6	0.3254
Milk testing			
(a) Regular	8	4	1.2387
(b) Not very regular	26	32	1.5279
(c) Very irregular	22	21	0.3420
(d) No opinion	4	3	0.2786
Payment for milk			
(a) Always in time	12	5	6.2579*
(b) Some times delayed	26	15	5.4308*
(c) Mostly delayed	20	38	7.5638*
(d) No opinion	2	2	0.0000
Supply of cattle feed			
(a) Regular	8	4	4.5004*
(b) Not very regular	35	24	3.7899*
(c) Very irregular	14	29	6.7899*
(d) No opinion	3	7	5.4332*

(Contd.)

Service and its quality	*STEP (n=60)*	*NON-STEP (n=60)*	*Absolute 'Z' value*
Quality of cattle feed			
Very good	4	2	0.9889
Good	37	28	2.5012*
Not satisfactory	10	20	5.7642*
No opinion	9	10	0.3750
Supply of fodder seeds			
Regular	5	3	0.5428
Not very regular	36	29	4.7856*
Very irregular	15	23	3.4786*
No opinion	4	5	0.3056
AI facility			
Regular	0	0	0.0000
Not very regular	24	17	3.0572*
Very irregular	31	39	2.7859*
No opinion	5	4	0.3254
Quality of AI			
Very good	0	0	0.0000
Good	15	11	1.2105
Not satisfactory	40	45	0.8592
No opinion	5	4	0.4321
Health care facilities			
Regular	4	4	0.0000
Not very regular	25	29	0.5465
Very irregular	24	17	3.9972*
No opinion	7	10	1.2954
Technical guidance			
Regular	25	7	15.3752*
Not very regular	22	16	8.5056*
Very irregular	9	29	10.8970*
No opinion	4	8	7.5222*

* Significant at 1% level.

Source: Calculated.

These employees work, on an average, for about 3.9 to 5.6 hours a day in Andhra Pradesh and Karnataka respectively. These people do attend other works in the remaining part of the day. Some have business, agriculture, petty trade, cycle shop, ration shop, vegetable shop, etc. Thus they make a living out of this meagre income. Productivity (average milk procurement/employee) of these employees is the highest (3148 litres/year) in STEP WDCSs of Karnataka followed by STEP WDCSs of Andhra Pradesh, NON-STEP WDCSs of Karnataka, and Andhra Pradesh.

Performance of WDCSs is also measured through services extended and quality of services provided by them and members were asked to give their opinion about each service. In all 10 such indicators were identified and the results are presented in Table 4.6. The standard normal deviate test ('z' test) indicated significant and positive differences in major indicators between STEP and NON-STEP WDCSs of Andhra Pradesh. Such indicators are regular payment for milk, regular supply supply of cattle feed, quality of cattle feed, supply of fodder seeds, AI and health care facilities, and technical guidance. It is to mention here that under STEP a revolving fund of Rs. 50,000 is kept in the account of WDCS and whenever there is a delay in payment from milk unions, WDCS paid milk bills from its own sources and adjusted it later while NON-STEP WDCSs have no much cushions. There is a considerable delay in payment at Chittoor, Prakasam, and Belgaum. Similarly, officials of milk unions have been arranging 10-12 training programmes to these (STEP) members and financial assistance was already paid by the Government of India. Thus, they are in a better position in terms of being new, having more resources, providing training, regular monitoring, and guidance. Put together, these factors contributed to superiority of STEP WDCSs over their counterparts in both states. Across states, dairying is taken as a profession in Karnataka and through sound financial management, and politics free environment youth are managing the WDCSs efficiently. Strong grass root level organisation made the other two tiers (union and federation) strong which in turn helped the primaries by paying remunerative prices and other technical inputs. This link is missing in Andhra Pradesh.

Table 4.7

Difference in Members' Perceptions Regarding Quality of Services Extended by WDCSs of Karnataka

Service and its quality	*STEP*	*NON-STEP*	*Absolute 'Z' value*
Milk collection			
(a) Regular	58	52	1.4376
(b) Not very regular	0	4	2.4890*
(c) Very irregular	0	0	0.0000
(d) No opinion	2	4	1.5628
Milk test			
Regular	10	10	0.0000
Not very regular	33	22	3.8978*
Very irregular	12	23	6.9815*
No opinion	5	5	0.0000
Payment for milk			
Always in time	58	55	1.3208
Some time delayed	2	2	0.0000
Mostly delayed	0	2	1.7651
No opinion	0	0	0.0000
Supply of cattle feed			
Regular	50	42	4.3895*
Not very regular	5	10	7.6345*
Very irregular	10	8	0.9856
No opinion	0	0	0.0000
Quality of cattle feed			
Very good	42	35	3.7540*
Good	10	12	1.2056
Not satisfactory	6	10	2.7809*
No opinion	2	3	0.7005

(Contd.)

Service and its quality	*STEP*	*NON-STEP*	*Absolute 'Z' value*
Supply of fodder seeds			
Regular	22	14	7.9007*
Not very regular	20	28	5.4328*
Very irregular	15	15	0.0000
No opinion	3	3	0.0000
AI facility			
Regular	36	24	3.5789*
Not very regular	14	17	0.8921
Very regular	5	15	8.6432*
No opinion	5	4	0.3256
Quality of AI			
Very good	28	12	7.2386*
Good	15	18	0.9862
Not satisfactory	15	22	3.7640*
No opinion	2	8	4.0876*
Healthcare facilities			
Regular	45	34	5.2089*
Not very regular	15	20	3.4322*
Very regular	0	6	4.3781*
No opinion	0	0	0.0000
Technical guidance			
Regular	55	3	15.3786*
Not very regular	5	25	5.6438*
Very irregular	0	32	12.3768*
No opinion	0	0	0.0000

* Significant at 1% level.

Source: Calculated.

Table 4.7 presents difference in members' perceptions of STEP and NON-STEP WDCSs in Karnataka. Once again, STEP WDCSs have performed well by delivering selected services and differences are significant in majority of the cases.

Table 4.8

Particulars of Fixed Assets (Rs. lakhs), 1999-00

Assets	*Andhra Pradesh*			*Karnataka*		
	STEP	*NON-STEP*	*Average*	*STEP*	*NON-STEP*	*Average*
Furniture	0.26	0.35	0.32	0.30	0.25	0.28
Land/buildings	0.18	0.42	0.31	0.29	0.36	0.32
Equipment	0.25	0.18	0.21	0.35	0.22	0.28
Others	0.15	0.10	0.13	0.24	0.15	0.20
Total	0.84	1.05	0.97	1.18	0.98	1.08

Source: Records of the selected WDCSs.

An attempt is also made to analyse the fixed assets owned by these WDCSs, state-wise. Assets included furniture, land/ buildings, dairy equipment, and others. Average value of assets/WDCSs of STEP in Andhra Pradesh is Rs. 0.84 lakhs while it is Rs. 1.18 lakhs in Karnataka. The value of assets in NON-STEP WDCSs of Andhra Pradesh is Rs. 1.05 lakhs while it is Rs. 0.98 lakhs in Karnataka. Thus, there are marginal differences in assets owned these WDCSs. On the whole, majority of these WDCSs are located in rented or government buildings. They have minimal furniture required for the maintenance of a WDCS.

Summary

An analysis of both qualitative and quantitative data on the performance of WDCSs revealed that WDCSs of Karnataka are superior to their counterparts in both states. It is mainly due to their homogeneous character, higher levels of awareness among producer members, management committee members, and employees. This was further strengthened by better financial position and support from the unions in terms of training and supervision. Members of these WDCSs were mainly satisfied by the services offered to them. Among all categories of WDCSs studied, NON-STOP WDCSs of Andhra Pradesh failed to live up to members expectation. Majority of the chairpersons of WDCSs are landlords drawn from high castes Hindus and election of chairperson is unanimous and ritualistic. Irrespective of the state, employment opportunities in these societies were cornered by well to do members having political affiliations leaving little scope for SCs/STs.

Chapter 5

Case Studies of Selected WDCSs

Previous chapter presented physical and financial performance of WDCSs at the aggregate level. An attempt is made in this chapter to provide a closer understanding, and appreciation at micro level and for this purpose case studies of a STEP and NON-STEP WDCSs each from Karnataka and Andhra Pradesh are presented here. Selection of the WDCSs presented is based on a mix of random procedure, impressions of the researcher, overall performance, members response, and cooperation during data collection. Names of WDCSs and members are changed, to some extent, to conceal their identity.

Somalapura STEP WDCSs

Somalapura is a dryland area located in Hoskote taluka of Rural Bangalore. Approach road to the village is bumpy and unfit for travel on rainy days. Bus stop is a kilometer away from the village. It has a primary school, and children have to walk for 7 kilometers to reach a high school. The village comprises of Vokkaligas, Kuruba, Reddy, Dhobi, and SC/ST. Prior to starting a WDCS in 1998, villagers were to walk for 4 kilometers to pour milk twice daily. Disadvantages of going to neighbouring village included walking long distances, ill-treatment by members of the host society, difficulty in carrying milk during rainy season, lack of safety and they were deprived of bonus and other benefits. During this period they maintained few local buffaloes and whatever surplus milk available was sent to neighbouring society. In the light of above difficulties, male members of the village decided to have a DCS. One of the members of this village has been working as extension officer in BAMUL. He informed villagers about the advantages of organising a STEP WDCS and encouraged his sister-in-law to take lead. Rukmanimma who only 'can sign' convinced her husband in organising a WDCS. Villagers too agreed to this proposal and STEP WDCS was organised on April 29, 1998. Extension officer from the BAMUL helped them in getting the required assistance under STEP alongwith training programmes for members and employees. Rukmanimma was unanimously elected as chairperson and management committee was constituted by drawing women from various families/castes. Unmarried ladies were selected as a secretary, and tester, and were given necessary training at Bangalore.

Collection of milk on the first day at the WDCSs was only 35 litres. Women decided to dispose of local buffaloes and brought crossbred cows from Chittoor. Slowly milk procurement started picking up and reached a peak of 350 litres/day. Committee meetings were conducted under the able guidance of lady supervisors regularly to review progress of the WDCS and corrective measures were initiated without time lag. All the members of the WDCS were trained in one or other program conducted by the BAMUL. Two members from this WDCS visited Amul too.

A word about secretary is in order here. She is a Vokkaliga and studied up to 11th standard. A good orator and having the quality of a leader. A word was sent to her on the previous day about our visit and she meticulously arranged the meeting. We reached the place as per the time given and she was present alongwith the tester and another member. All the records were up to date and neatly maintained. Siron was blown giving information about our arrival and women one by one reached the WDCS at a frequency of an hour. That gave us sufficient time to discuss individually about their views, problems, and suggestions. The women were so hospitable that they had not allowed us without talking breakfast as also lunch. Their grievances included muddy and bumpy road, a high school, and protected water scheme.

Table 5.1

Bovine Population

Age	*Crossbred cows*	*Local cows*	*Murrah/ Mehsana*	*Local buffaloes*
1. Males over 3 years	0	26	0	0
2. Females over 3 years	50	16	5	10
3. Males below 3 years	2	0	0	0
4. Females below 3 years	20	14	4	0
Total	72	56	9	10

Source: Records of the WDCS.

Physical and financial performance of the WDCS is presented in the following paragraphs. It has seventy two crossbred cows and fifty six local cows (Table 5.1). Of the local cattle, majorities of them are bullocks. There are few buffaloes too, but discussion with women indicated that they decided to dispose them, and planning to purchase crossbreds as early as possible.

Table 5.2

Composition of Membership, 1999-00

Sr. No.	*Caste*	*Women*
1.	Vokkaliga	42
2.	Kuruba	19
3.	SC	15
4.	ST	14
5.	Dhobi	08
6.	Reddy	05
	Total	103

Source: Records of the WDCS.

Table 5.3

Management Committee Members

Names (Smt.)	Age	Years of schooling	Caste	No. of years on committee
1. Rukmanimma	35	0	Vokkaliga	3 years
2. Radhama	22	6	Vokkaliga	3 years
3. Shusheelamma	30	7	Vokkaliga	3 years
4. Muniamma	55	9	Vokkaliga	3 years
5. Devamma	35	10	Vokkaliga	3 years
6. Anasuyamma	37	0	Dhobi	3 years
7. Anjanamma	65	5	Reddy	3 years
8. Rajayamma	50	2	Kuruba	3 years
9. Parvatamma	35	0	SC	3 years

Source: Records of the WDCS.

The society has 103 members of which 41% are Vokkaligas. Kuruba, SC/ST, Dhobi, and Reddys are other communities on the membership. Most of the management committee members are educated while chairperson has no formal education (Table 5.3). However, she found to be intelligent and organising. She succeeded in increasing the crossbreds, enhancing procurement, and trying her best to conduct fat test twice daily. Not even a single complaint was reported against her honesty. Most of the time she spends own money regarding WDCS's work. Husband and children are understanding and extending necessary support for her active participation in the meetings of WDCS. She took pains in learning to sign and would like to read and write too. As mentioned earlier, Vokkaligas constituted 41% of the membership but they occupied 56% of the posts on management committee. Thus, Kurubas are denied their due share on the committee. Kurubas represent backward caste while Vokkaligas are forward caste.

Table 5.4

Attendance in Monthly Committee Meetings

Month	*1998*	*1999*	*2000*
January	0	6	7
February	0	6	7
March	0	6	7
April	9	8	0
May	7	8	0
June	8	6	0
July	8	9	7
August	0	7	8
September	7	6	0
October	8	7	6
November	9	6	7
December	8	7	8

Source: Records of the WDCS.

Attendance in monthly meetings is extremely good which speaks about the members involvement (Table 5.4). Agenda is circulated a week in advance and women participate in meetings without support of the men folk. Discussions with committee members revealed that women do not consider it necessary to inform their husbands about the meeting or the contents. Men too felt society is women's business and they never entered the premises. Meetings last for about an hour and half and the issues discussed are: collection, amounts paid, profit, supply of technical inputs, purchase of crossbreds through bank finance, selection of members for training, etc. These meetings are lively and conducted in a congenial atmosphere. Meetings were not conducted on two occasion (August 1998, and September 2000) as majority of the members were on training.

Table 5.5

Progress of the Society

Content	*1998-99*	*1999-00*
1. Members	103	103
2. Procurement (litres)	79687	109821
3. Amount paid to producers (Rs. lakhs)	6.77	9.33
4. Net profit (rupees)	50000	61080
5. Cattle feed (tonnes)	25.5	36.2
6. AIs done	45	56
7. First aid	35	40
8. Annual expenditure (Rs. lakhs)	0.19	0.25

Source: Records of the WDCS.

Progress of the society is given in Table 5.5. There is no increase in membership and there is hardly any possibility too. Milk procurement increased from about 80000 litres in 1998-99 to 1.10 lakh litres in 1999-00. During the last two years, society distributed Rs. 16 lakhs. Other inputs supplied are also in tune with the milk procurement. The society has a reserve fund of Rs. 1.00 lakh and has assets worth of Rs. 38000. The members propose to purchase 35 crossbreds in the coming year so that they can supply 500-600 litres/day.

They would like to be highest suppliers to the union which would enable them to get an award. They also propose to have public toilets for women, all weather approach road, and PHC in the village. The society started two SHGs covering 36 members. They meet once fortnightly and contribute Rs. 50 / member as saving. These SHGs are 12 months old. The groups also started lending for purposes like health, school fees, petty trade, sewing machines, social functions, etc. There is 100% recovery and they would like to link them to a nationalised bank. Looking at the overall progress and amount of awareness created among women, Eanadu TV prepared a 30 minutes serial about the WDCS which was telecasted on Eanadu Kannada channel. WDCS has been centre of attraction to many VIPs visiting KMF.

Kotamaranahalli NON-STEP WDCS

Kotamaranahalli is relatively a big village situated in Chennapattna taluka of Bangalore. It is 65 kilometers away from Bangalore on the way to Mysore. It has 184 households with 798 population. The village has 215 acres of irrigated land, source being canal. This area is famous for coconut gardens, paddy, and vegetables. Few farmers exclusively cultivate green fodder and sale it is the market. There are 269 bovines of which 78 are crossbreds 'in milk' (Table 5.6). Average yield of a crossbred is 8-10 litres/day as against 2 litres/day for a local cow, and 3 litres/day for a local buffalo in the area. The village has many facilities like bus stop, market, high school, PHC, PACS, youth club, and mahila mandal.

BAMUL thought of organising a WDCSs in 1991 and a senior official who hails from the village informed them about the news. A gramsabha was called for and was decided to organise a WDCS in the village. Till that time, milk vendors were the only source of procurement who cheated them on several pretexts. The decision of the gramsabha was informed to the union and thus started a WDCS. The union provided a grant of Rs. 5000, four milk cans, and testing equipment free of cost, no other facility was provided later. Thus, it became the first WDCS organised under BAMUL. The chairperson who was elected in 1991 continued till 1998, and a new chairperson was elected subsequently.

Table 5.6
Bovine Population

Age	*Crossbred cows*	*Local cows*	*Local buffaloes*
1. Males over 3 years	2	15	0
2. Females over 3 years	78	35	40
3. Males below 3 years	5	0	0
4. Females below 3 years	42	20	26
Total	127	70	66

Source: Records of the WDCS.

Table 5.7

Composition of Membership, 1999-2000

Sl. No.	*Caste*	*Women*
1.	Vokkaliga	169
2.	SC	68
3.	ST	3
4.	Dhobi	1
	Total	241

Source: Records of the WDCS.

Though there is change in the composition of the committee members, secretary, tester, and helper continued till date (all of them are women). Secretary hails from the neighbouring village and with the help of her husband organised a PACS in her village. Looking at the success of the PACS, she alongwith the members of WDCS would like to organise a multipurpose society so that they can undertake PDS, and manufacturing silk. Her husband who works for KSRTC has some clout and is prepared to help organising the new society too.

Table 5.8

Management Committee Members

Name (Smt.)	*Age*	*Years of schooling*	*Caste*	*No. of years on committee*
1. Chandramma	40	8	Vokkaliga	8 years
2. Shusheelamma	46	9	Vokkaliga	10 years
3. Sunandamma	45	8	Vokkaliga	6 years
4. Jayamma	50	0	Vokkaliga	6 years
5. Kalyanamma	54	0	Vokkaliga	2 years
6. Pratisha	30	10	Vokkaliga	2 years
7. Sakamma	40	0	Vokkaliga	2 years
8. Lakshmamma	35	10	Vokkaliga	2 years
9. Chikodamma	50	2	SC	2 years

Source: Records of the WDCS.

The WDCS has a membership of 240 (Table 5.7), and Vokkaligas constitute 70% followed by SC (28%). As regards composition of committee members (Table 5.8), about 89% of posts are occupied by Vokkaligas leaving one seat to SCs. About half of them were elected in 1998. Committee meetings are conducted, nevertheless, regularly and the attendance is satisfactory (Table 5.9). Discussions in committee meetings centered around sour milk, measures to motive members to supply quality milk, and fat/milk losses during transit. Testing is not regular in the society. Annual general body meetings are conducted regularly and the attendance is ranging between 55-72%.

Table 5.9

Attendance in Monthly Committee Meetings

Year	*Jan*	*Feb*	*Mar*	*Apr*	*May*	*June*	*July*	*Aug*	*Sept*	*Oct*	*Nov*	*Dec*
1991	0	0	0	0	0	0	0	6	0	0	0	5
1992	0	0	0	0	6	0	0	6	5	7	0	7
1993	0	6	9	0	7	0	9	7	8	8	6	0
1994	6	0	5	6	6	5	6	5	6	6	6	7
1995	5	0	5	6	7	7	8	6	6	6	6	5
1996	5	7	6	5	5	0	5	6	5	7	5	9
1997	5	8	0	9	6	6	0	6	6	8	7	5
1998	5	4	3	6	0	6	5	5	6	7	6	5
1999	5	5	6	8	5	5	0	6	0	0	8	5
2000	6	5	5	5	0	0	6	5	5	5	5	5

Source: Records of the WDCS.

Table 5.10
Progress of the Society

Year	*Members*	*Procurement (lakh litres)*	*Milk Sold in village (litres)*	*Amount paid to producers (Rs. lakhs)*	*Net profit (Rs. lakhs)*	*Price difference (Rs.)*	*Bonus distributed (Rs.)*	*Sour milk (litres)*
1990-91	133	0.29	400	1.88	0.04	0	0	200
1991-92	151	0.29	450	1.96	0.05	0	0	0
1992-93	151	0.94	350	5.59	0.19	0	0	0
1993-94	151	0.79	375	5.94	0.06	0	0	0
1994-95	157	1.17	400	9.05	0.60	0	0	0
1995-96	157	1.37	250	10.95	0.29	4000	9663	0
1996-97	180	2.00	400	16.61	0.08	32000	27100	0
1997-98	189	1.64	370	13.98	0.39	28000	77100	664
1998-99	231	1.70	375	15.29	0.88	24000	31713	1761
1999-00	240	1.93	400	18.87	0.80	53000	0	0

Source: Records of the WDCS.

Table 5.11
Service Rendered by the Society

Year	*Cattle feed (tonnes)*	*AIs done*	*Contribution to village (Rs. lakhs)*	*Annual expenditure (Rs. lakhs)*
1990-91	3.62	0	0.00	0.07
1991-92	3.80	45	0.02	0.08
1992-93	13.15	50	0.03	0.17
1993-94	11.69	65	0.04	0.22
1994-95	16.11	60	0.03	0.21
1995-96	20.53	56	0.02	0.27
1996-97	32.02	85	0.03	0.46
1997-98	22.20	80	0.02	0.41
1998-99	23.27	75	0.03	0.48
1999-00	26.76	70	0.04	0.42

Source: Records of the WDCS.

The society had a spectacular progress in membership, procurement, and other indicators considered (Table 5.10). Membership increased from 133 in 1990-91 to 240 in 1999-00, while procurement from 0.29 lakh litres to 1.93 lakh litres during the same period. Milk sold in the village hovered around 400 litres/year. It posted net profits throughout the study period and distributed bonus too during 1996-99. WDCS has a reserve fund of Rs. 43635 and purchased plot for construction of own building (at the moment it is in a rented building paying Rs. 250/month). The society has been contributing to village amenities (Table 5.11). Thus, the overall process is satisfactory.

Majority of the members of the WDCS were not trained. When inquired about the facilities extended, they were unhappy because many STEP WDCSs started oflate have been getting lot of assistance while they were not provided such financial help. They wanted to start three SHGs, adult education programmes for women, and a multipurpose society. They also informed that union should arrange training programmes to its members, secretary, tester, and helper. Most of the committee members are determined in their plans.

Nagaram STEP WDCS

Nagaram is located in Lingala Ghanapur mandal of Warangal district. It has 156 households with 950 population. Total cultivated area of the village is ha. 594 of which ha. 125 is irrigated through borewells and tubewells. Jawar, paddy, maize and few fodder crops are grown in this area. It has a primary school and well maintained approach road. The village has 42 crossbreds, 515 local cows, 255 improved buffaloes, and 296 local buffaloes (Table 5.12). Due to acute fodder scarcity, yields of these animals are low. Men folk of this village tried thrice (1986, 1991, and 1995) to organise a DCS. They did run a DCS for few months but were forced to close it due to internal clashes and feuds. As there was no assured outlet for milk, women of the village have been facing lot of problems in carrying milk to neighbouring village, and were cheated by few milk vendors. Young women of the village decided, in the later part of 1997, to organise a WDCS. They met manager of the nearby milk chilling centre who readily agreed to provide necessary support. Manager in turn consulted the milk union and tried his best to get a STEP WDCS in this village. He alongwith his field supervisors twice visited the village and organised a gramsabha and got it resolved to have a WDCS. Men of the village too supported this idea because: (a) their earlier efforts failed thrice, and (b) there is financial assistance, and technical guidance under STEP. Thus, started the WDCS with 135 women members.

Table 5.12
Bovine Population

Age	*Crossbred cows*	*Local cows*	*Murrah/ Mehsaha*	*Local buffaloes*
1. Males over 3 years	0	240	0	15
2. Females over 3 years	25	155	145	175
3. Males below 3 years	2	15	15	20
4. Females below 3 years	15	105	95	86
Total	42	515	255	296

Source: Records of the WDCS.

Composition of the membership (1999-00) is presented in Table 5.13. Out of 142, 40 are Reddys, 72 BCs (Gowda, Kapu, Dhobi, and Yadav), and rest are SCs. Mrs. A. Radha who studied 12th standard, was selected as a chairperson. Mrs. Radha's husband is a landlord in the village who always involved himself in the social, and cultural activities. Attendance in committee meetings is as expected the reason being most of the members are small and marginal (Table 5.15). WDCS noticed reasonable progress in procurement, amount paid to producers, and net profits. However, supply of cattlefeed, and fodder seeds is not in proportion to milk procurement. Milk is collected once in a day in this society and the testing is not carried out regularly. When asked about the reasons for not conducting the fat test, committee members expressed satisfaction with the current lactometer reading. However, when informed about the lively disadvantages, they agreed to make it compulsory.

Table 5.13

Composition of Membership, 1999-00

Sr. No.	*Caste*	*Women*
1.	Reddy	40
2.	BC	72
3.	SC	30
4.	Total	142

Source: Records of the WDCS .

Table 5.14

Management Committee Members

	Name (Smt.)	*Age*	*Years of schooling*	*Caste*	*No. of years on committee*
1.	A. Radha	40	12	Reddy	2 years
2.	A. Saroja	35	8	Reddy	2 years
3.	G. Venkatamma	50	9	Reddy	2 years
4.	B. Lakshmi	45	6	BC	2 years
5.	V. Lakshmi	50	7	BC	2 years
6.	G. Anjanamma	28	8	BC	2 years
7.	M. Padma	45	8	BC	3 years
8.	J. Ellamma	50	2	SC	2 years
9.	T. Padma	35	3	Kapu	2 years

Source: Records of the WDCS.

Members wanted that they be given feed at subsidies rates and distribution of crossbreds to BCs and FCs too. Under the existing norms of the Government of Andhra Pradesh, SC/ST corporation and DRDAs provide subsidy-cum-loan facilities to SCs/STs. Members of other communities are against this policy. They complained that the recovery is poor from SCs/STs members. Most of the SCs/STs who took loans were defaulters and banks are not coming forward to provide fresh loans. Members who took loans are supplying to private traders.

They were very appreciative of the manager who helped them in getting STEP WDCS. He is an young and energetic person who has a lot of enthusiasm to help farmers. During our visits to these societies, there were few showers and farmers requested for jawar seeds. Soon after reaching chilling centre manager completed the necessary formalities to get seeds from Hyderabad. However there was some delay during transit followed by two holidays. As the soil is getting dry farmers rushed to chilling centre for seeds. On inquiry manager came to know about the arrival of seeds at private transport agency but he was yet to get the necessary delivery forms through post. Since farmers were pressing and it is getting late to sow seeds, manager approached the transport agency, gave personal surity of Rs. 10000 and got the seeds distributed without further delay. On receiving the seeds, farmers visited chilling centre to convey their thanks and appreciation. Manager was happy to have honoured his promise.

Table 5.15

Attendance in Monthly Committee Meetings

Month	*1998*	*1999*	*2000*
January	0	6	8
February	0	6	8
March	0	7	8
April	0	7	8
May	5	6	5
June	7	7	5
July	8	8	5
August	5	5	6
September	4	5	6
October	5	4	6
November	6	4	5
December	7	4	5

Source: Records of the WDCS

Konakanamitla WDCS

Konakanamitla (Prakasam district) is a big village and mandal head quarters too. It is 65 kilometers away from Ongole. It has 420 house holds and 4200 population. The village has ha.

820 dryland and tobacco, jawar, redgram, and bajra are cultivated. Thus, drinking water, and fodder are the major problems of the area. Droughts are very common in this part of the district. As there are few employment opportunities in the village/district, men folk migrate to urban centres like Vijayawada, Guntur, and Tirupati for gainful employment. Frequent failures of monsoons as also migration of men put immense pressure on women. All the wells in the village are dried up and women are to walk 2-4 kilometers daily to fetch two pots of drinking water. In addition, they are also to take care of 1-2 local buffaloes purchased either with bank loan or owned by their husbands. Since dry fodder too is not available, either it is purchased, if possible, or collected from neighbouring fields during odd hours. Added to it, maintaining the family (children, aged, and handicapped) is the responsibility of women. Thus, women of the area carry the entire work load of agriculture, animal husbandry, and household chores.

Table 5.16

Progress of the Society

Content	*1997-98*	*1998-99*	*1999-00*
1. Members	135	136	142
2. Procurement (litres)	28430	60300	70250
3. Milk sold in village (litres)	1400	2500	3164
4. Amount paid to producers (Rs. lakhs)	2.56	5.78	6.07
5. Net Profit (Rs. lakhs)	0.13	0.25	0.30
6. Cattle feed (kgs.)	85	142	185
7. Seeds	120	150	240
8. *Animals financed*			
(a) Cows	20	35	45
(b) Buffaloes	15	40	40
9. Annual expenditure (Rs. lakhs)	0.08	0.12	0.12

Source: Records of the WDCS.

The water available in this area has floured content and this village was covered under project covered by the Government of Netherlands (for more details, see Chapter 1). When society was organised, each member got 250 kgs of feed on subsidy basis, 50 crossbreds animals were provided to SCs/STs, and 64 steel milk cans were distributed. Apart from this, managerial subsidy, a grant of Rs. 10000, and office furniture too were provided.

Table 5.17

Bovine Population

	Age	*Local buffaloes*
1.	Males over 3 years	150
2.	Females over 3 years	1250
3.	Males below 3 years	120
4.	Females below 3 years	520
	Total	2040

Source: Records of the WDCS.

Table 5.18

Composition of Membership, 1999-00

Sl. No.	*Caste*	*Women*
1.	Reddy	212
2.	BC	41
3.	SC	8
4.	ST	2
	Total	263

Source: Records of the WDCS

Prior to 1992, there was no DCS in the village. Women used to prepare butter/ghee and sold in the Ongole town. Situation improved soon after organisation the WDCS in 1992. Women felt happy and its being run satisfactorily since then. However, things worsened soon after withdrawal of government support in 1995. Since it is a big village, having number of castes, organising them has been a problem. As a result, three private dairymen are thriving in the village. They collect as much as

250-300 litres/day. They pay regularly and 20-25 paise more than the WDCS price. Further, they provide hand loans to purchase feeds, animals and giving steel cans/sarees/glasses etc. as gifts. Society has been functioning for the last 9 years without break. During this period, it purchased a plot worth of Rs. 35000 and got a building constructed (it was yet to be inaugurated). Currently, the WDCS is in a rented room paying Rs. 300/- month.

Table 5.19

Management Committee Members

	Name (Smt.)	*Age*	*Years of schooling*	*Caste*	*No. of years on committee*
1.	P. Akkamma	45	5	Reddy	10 years
2.	V. Subbamma	44	illiterate	Reddy	10 years
3.	P. Venkatalakshmamma	46	illiterate	Reddy	10 years
4.	R. Ramalakshmi	42	illiterate	Reddy	10 years
5.	W. Chandramma	42	illiterate	Reddy	10 years
6.	P. Obulamma	44	illiterate	Reddy	10 years
7.	V. Subbamma	39	illiterate	Reddy	10 years
8.	R. Rajyalakshmi	52	illiterate	Reddy	10 years
9.	S. Bharati	48	illiterate	Reddy	10 years

Source: Records of the WDCS.

The chairperson of the WDCS has 25 acres of land and all her family members (4 daughters, son, and husband) are supportive. She is being continued as a chairperson since 1992. She visited Anand twice and attended meetings at Ongole, Vijayawada, and Chittoor. The village has over 2000 local buffaloes (Table 5.17) of which 1250 are females above three years. Improved buffaloes and crossbreds are not maintained due to scarcity of water, and fodder. There are 263 members and 81% of them are Reddys (Table 5.18) and all the positions on the management committee were occupied by Reddys only (Table 5.19). Except chairperson, all the committee members are illiterate and are being continued since inception.

Their involvement in the committee meetings has been minimum. Meetings were conducted as a formality. Chairperson and the secretary are the key members who took decisions regarding the WDCS, rest of them are mostly spectators. On an average, 4-5 meetings/year were conducted and the attendance in committee meetings (Table 5.20), and annual general body meetings was 35-45%.

Table 5.20

Attendance in Monthly Committee Meetings

Month	*1992*	*1993*	*1994*	*1995*	*1996*	*1997*	*1998*	*1999*	*2000*
January	5	4	7	5	6	6	7	6	6
February	0	0	5	4	7	6	7	6	0
March	4	0	0	5	0	6	7	0	5
April	5	0	0	5	0	0	0	7	0
May	0	6	4	0	5	0	5	0	0
June	0	0	4	0	5	0	0	8	5
July	0	5	0	7	5	4	8	0	0
August	6	8	7	5	4	6	0	4	5
September	0	0	0	6	0	0	8	0	0
October	5	0	0	0	0	0	0	6	5
November	0	0	0	0	5	5	9	0	5
December	0	7	8	3	5	6	7	6	0

Source: Records of the WDCS.

Collection timings are 5.00-6.00 am and 6.00-630 pm. Though there is increase in membership from 181 in 1992-93 to 268 in 1999-00, procurement never crossed a lakh litres/year. It is mainly due to presence of two political parties in the village. Heritage dairy has been offering relatively higher prices and half the members are pouring their milk to heritage. Further, as mentioned earlier, heritage has been providing a number of services to its members. Being a private dairy they have less over-head expenses, centrally located plant, efficient management, quick decision making process, prompt payment, etc. Further, they are luring some of union's employees by paying heavy salaries, commission, gifts and above all using caste, and party cards. Thus, the cooperative is facing problems.

The society posted net profits throughout the study period.

Table 5.21
Progress of the Society

Year	*Members*	*Procurement (lakh litres)*	*Milk sold in village (rupees)*	*Amount paid to producers*	*Net profit (rupees) (Rs. lakhs)*
1992-93	181	0.42	2020	2.50	26730
1993-94	205	0.40	9932	3.00	10547
1994-95	226	0.34	20310	2.10	11290
1995-96	226	0.54	51407	4.00	17159
1996-97	253	0.91	96907	7.50	49603
1997-98	253	1.00	43500	10.50	30930
1998-99	253	0.94	68642	9.50	743
1999-00	268	0.66	53435	6.94	7860

Source: Records of the WDCS.

Table 5.22
Services Rendered by the Society

Year	*Cattle feed (tonnes)*	*Seeds (rupees)*	*Annual expenditure (Rs. lakhs)*
1992-93	0.26	400	0.08
1993-94	0.35	405	0.22
1994-95	0.11	405	0.18
1995-96	0.72	1305	0.27
1996-97	1.42	3033	0.35
1997-98	5.30	1120	0.57
1998-99	5.30	2348	0.74
1999-00	6.25	2400	0.87

Source: Records of the WDCS.

WDCS provided few technical inputs (seed, and cattle feed). When inquired, members informed that feed is of poor quality, and price is expensive hence most of them are purchasing from outside. Chairperson informed her unhappiness with the members because they are supplying good quality milk to private dairy and low quality to WDCS. She is afraid of competition from private dairy. Some of the villagers still have faith in her and hence pouring milk in WDCS, otherwise it would have been closed by now. Half of her family members are supplying to private dairy and threatening her to close the WDCS.

Members wanted to distribute reserve fund as bonus. However, she instead to construct building on the site purchased. When nobody came forward to take up the contract, chairperson took up the contract and completed work on time. Some more funds are required to finish the work. Procurement on the day of visit was 130 liters with 10 litres as a local sales (for more details on WDCSs of Andhra Pradesh see, Rao, 1998).

Summary

Close observation of four cases studies reveal interesting results. In two out of four WDCSs, an official who hailed from the village informed women about WDCS and helped in getting necessary financial support. Though initially men folk were reluctant, they agreed to organise a WDCS as funds available under STEP, and their previous experiments failed. Thus, women organised WDCSs with the help of union's officials and men folk. Having entered the business organisations they managed it on sound financial management principles. Young and educated women from high caste Hindus managed to occupy the positions on management committees. As observed in chapter 4, STEP societies are better managed compared to NON-STEP societies. Further, performance of WDCSs of Karnataka is much better than WDCSs of Andhra Pradesh. The WDCS of Karnataka supplied a number of production enhancement inputs than the WDCSs of Andhra Pradesh. In general, women faced number of problems from emerging private dairies and sleeping membership. Further, these problems were compounded by presence of political parties and caste groups.

Chapter 6

An Overview of Selected Respondents

This chapter focuses attention on an overview of selected respondents participating in both STEP and NON-STEP WDCSs. Parameters considered include land, and animal holdings, distribution of members according to caste and education, their association with society's activities, participation in decision making process, sources of knowledge about village organisations, and perceptions about impact of WDCSs on their lives. The details are arranged under three sub-headings: (a) socio-economic status of respondents, (b) decision making process of women, and (c) impact of WDCSs on women.

Socio-economic Status of Respondents

As mentioned in Chapter 1, respondents were selected from 24 WDCSs each from Andhra Pradesh and Karnataka representing different agro-climatic, and socio-economic backgrounds with varying land and animal holdings covering STEP and NON-STEP WDCSs. An attempt is made in this section to describe socio-economic status of the respondents.

Tables 6.1 to 6.4 presents composition of membership according to land and animal holdings. On the whole, a quarter of the respondents belong to landless category across states and a third of them are marginal farmers. Thus, more than half of the respondents are either landless or marginal farmers in Andhra Pradesh and Karnataka. Similarly, 25-40% of the households have one animal. Thus, majority of the landless households maintained one animal. Such an observation has an economic logic. Landless and marginal farmers also work as wage labours and at the end of working day, they collect some weeds/grass on bunds/bushes, and tree tops while coming home. There is also a practice of landlord allowing them to carry a head load of green fodder/dry fodder. In the absence of village common grazing lands these people find it difficult to maintain more animals.

Table 6.1

Composition of Membership According to Land and Animal Holding in STEP WDCSs of Andhra Pradesh

Land holding (ha)	*1 animal*	*2 animals*	*3 animals*	*4 and above*	*Total*
Landless	13 (76.5)	4 (23.5)	0 (0.0)	0 (0.0)	17 (100.0
0.1-1.0	7 (35.0)	6 (30.0)	5 (25.0)	2 (10.0)	20 (100.0)
1.1-2.0	4 (36.4)	5 (45.4)	2 (18.2)	0 (0.0)	11 (100.0)
2.1-4.0	0 (0.0)	2 (28.6)	4 (57.1)	1 (14.3)	7 (100.0)
4.1 and above	0 (0.0)	2 (40.0)	3 (60.0)	0 (0.0)	5 (100.0)
Total	24 (40.0)	19 (31.7)	14 (23.3)	3 (5.0)	60 (100.0)

(Figures in parentheses are percentages to row totals).

Source: Field study.

Further, because of their preoccupation with wage labour, they can not afford maintaining more animals. Most of the time it is the girls/boys who took care of these animals in their absence. Large farmers constituted 8-12% of the total sample and most of them owned three animals. This speaks about their ability to supply feeds, fodder, and other inputs required for maintenance of animals. The two assets (land and animals) represent the economic status of rural households. Higher the assets higher the status and they go with caste too. However, caste-wise and land/animal-wise distribution is not presented here. It is to be mentioned here that land is mostly owned by the husbands. It is not customary to have land in the name of women in rural India, mostly land is passed on to sons while some durable consumer goods are given to daughters at the time of marriage.

Table 6.2

Composition of Membership According to Land and Animal Holding in NON-STEP WDCSs of Andhra Pradesh

Land holding (ha)	*1 animal*	*2 animals*	*3 animals*	*4 and above*	*Total*
landless	10 (66.7)	5 (33.3)	0 (0.0)	0 (0.0)	15 (100.0)
0.1-1.0	9 (50.0)	8 (44.4)	1 (5.6)	0 (0.0)	18 (100.0)
1.1-2.0	1 (8.3)	6 (50.0)	3 (25.0)	2 (16.7)	12 (100.0)
2.1-4.0	1 (12.5)	2 (25.0)	3 (37.5)	2 (25.0)	8 (100.0)
4.1 and above	0 (0.0)	3 (42.9)	3 (42.9)	1 (14.2)	7 (100.0)
Total	21 (35.0)	24 (40.0)	10 (16.7)	5 (8.3)	60 (100.0)

(Figures in parentheses are percentages to row totals).

Source: Field study.

Table 6.3

Composition of Membership According to Land and Animal Holding in STEP WDCSs of Karnataka

Land holding (ha)	*1 animal*	*2 animals*	*3 animals*	*4 and above*	*Total*
landless	14	5	2	0	21
	(66.7)	(23.8)	(9.5)	(0.0)	(100.0)
0.1-1.0	6	10	4	0	20
	(30.0)	(50.0)	(20.0)	(0.0)	(100.0)
1.1-2.0	1	4	3	1	9
	(11.1)	(44.5)	(33.3)	(11.1)	(100.0)
2.1-4.0	1	4	3	2	10
	(10.0)	(40.0)	(30.0)	(20.0)	(100.0)
4.1 and above	0	0	0	0	0
	(0.0)	(0.0)	(0.0)	(0.0)	(0.0)
Total	22(36.7)	23(38.3)	12(20.0)	3(5.0)	60(100.0)

(*Note :* Figures in parentheses are percentages to row totals).
Source: Field study.

Table 6.4

Composition of Membership According to Land and Animal Holding in NON-STEP WDCSs of Karnataka

Land holding (ha)	*1 animal*	*2 animals*	*3 animals*	*4 and above*	*Total*
landless	7	6	2	0	15
	(46.7)	(40.0)	(13.3)	(0.0)	(100.0)
0.1-1.0	6	10	3	0	19
	(31.6)	(52.6)	(15.8)	(0.0)	(100.0)
1.1-2.0	2	6	3	1	12
	(16.7)	(50.0)	(25.0)	(8.3)	(100.0)
2.1-4.0	0	4	3	1	8
	(0.0)	(50.0)	(37.5)	(12.5)	(100.0)
4.1 and above	0	2	2	2	6
	(0.0)	(33.3)	(33.3)	(33.4)	(100.0)
Total	15	28	13	4	60
	(25.0)	(46.7)	(21.7)	(6.6)	(100.0)

(*Note :* Figures in parentheses are percentages to row totals).
Source: Field study.

An inquiry into the ownership of land and animals revealed interesting results. As much as 8.3-16.7% of respondents mentioned ownership of some land on their name while 23.3-56.7% of have reported ownership of animals (Table 6.5). There is a practice in southern India that high caste, land holding Hindus give dowry in the form of land, cash, jewelry, and household articles. It is given as a status symbol also as security at the time of old age/desertion/widowhood. In some places, it is to escape from land ceiling act. Similarly, women of other castes get animals (depending upon their position) at the time of marriage. There are instances of purchasing animals out of their own savings too. Thus, the results are in tune with prevailing social customs.

Table 6.5

Ownership of Land and Animals (%) among Sample Respondents

State/Category	*Land*	*Animals*
Andhra Pradesh		
STEP (n=60)	16.7	40.0
NON-STEP (n=60)	13.3	23.3
Karnataka		
STEP (n=60)	10.0	56.7
NON-STEP (n=60)	8.3	43.3

Source: Field study.

Table 6.6 presents details on age, caste, education, etc. of the women respondents. Average age is about 42 years in Andhra Pradesh while it is 33.3 in Karnataka. Across various categories of WDCSs, average age of women belonged to STEP societies is less than that of NON-STEP societies. Reasons for these differences are already explained in Chapter 4. Caste-wise, FCs and SCs/STs constituted 30% each followed by BCs in Andhra Pradesh while the proportion of BCs is slightly on the higher side in Karnataka. Nevertheless, similar composition is noticed in both Andhra Pradesh and Karnataka.

Table 6.6

Socio-economic Status of Sample Respondents

Particulars	*Andhra Pradesh*			*Karnataka*		
	STEP (n=60)	*NON-STEP (n=60)*	*Average (n=120)*	*STEP (n=60)*	*NON-STEP*	*Average (n=120)*
Age	37.5	48.5	42.1	29.7	36.9	33.3
Average size of the family	5.3	5.7	5.5	4.8	5.5	5.2
Caste						
FC (%)	28.3	30.0	28.9	20.0	23.3	22.1
BC (%)	43.4	40.0	41.4	53.3	50.0	51.5
SC/ST (%)	28.3	30.0	28.7	26.7	26.7	26.4
Education						
illiterate (%)	13.3	18.3	16.3	11.7	16.7	15.1
can sign (%)	18.3	20.0	18.9	16.7	18.3	17.1
1-5 (%)	36.7	40.0	38.4	36.7	40.0	38.3
6-10 (%)	16.7	15.0	15.8	18.2	15.0	17.7
11 and above (%)	15.0	6.7	10.6	16.7	10.0	12.5
Average total income (Rs./annum)	22040	14580	18310	29375	20585	24980
% of income from dairying	25.34	17.25	22.30	36.43	22.07	31.84

Source: Field study.

In this era of information, importance of education needs no mention. Both formal and non-formal education would be essential for rural women. For those disadvantaged groups who failed to get a chance to go to school during childhood, adult education is the alternative. These classes are being conducted by government, NGOs, social, and cultural organisations. According to Freire (1970), education is essential for creating awareness among the people. Interestingly, majority of the respondents are literate. However, concentration is in 1-5 years of schooling. Women who 'can sign' constituted as much as 17% of the total respondents and in majority of the cases credit goes to WDCSs. These societies have been organising adult education classes in leisure time (mostly nights) and women are now happy to say that they can sign due to the efforts of WDCSs. Further, there is a stigma associated with illiteracy these days. Thus, more and more women are participating in these classes and taking the helping of their daughters/sons too so as to enable them to sign.

Average total income of these families is Rs. 18,130 in Andhra Pradesh and Rs. 24,980 in Karnataka while members of STEP WDCSs reported relatively higher incomes. This higher income is partly contributed by additional income from dairying (Table 6.6) and commercialization of agriculture in these families.

Success of an organisation depends, to a large extent, on enlightened, enthusiastic, and loyal membership. Members participation in economic activities of the organisation is a must for its viability and sustainability. Sleeping and inactive membership in no membership. Higher percentages of involvement is reported from STEP WDCSs of Karnataka than their counterparts of the study (Table 6.7). There is a need to bring awareness about services provided by WDCSs and all out efforts, on a continuous basis, should be made to involve all the members. Low levels of involvement could be also due to enrolling more than one member from a single family. Such procedure keeps membership on high side but its impact on turnover of the WDCSs is minimal. Such practices are followed keeping in view of the elections but should be discouraged. Attendance in general body once again gives true picture about members involvement. This is too low in Andhra Pradesh which needs to be stepped up. A sinking and weak organisation can not command members loyalty. Turnovers would be low due to non-involvement, which further disassociates members from the organisation. This is a vicious circle. In such circumstances, all members should come together and forego something in the initial period till organisation is viable and healthy. Once healthy, WDCS can meet requirements/aspirations of members. Hence, a close monitoring of the health of WDCSs is essential.

Table 6.7

Members Association with Society's Activities

Particulars	*Andhra Pradesh*			*Karnataka*		
	STEP	*NON-STEP*	*Average*	*STEP*	*NON-STEP*	*Average*
1. Members	53	95	75	85	65	75
2. Pourer members (%)	44.6	34.2	29.2	68.5	50.4	57.2
3. Purchasing feeds (%)	30.3	25.0	25.6	52.8	38.5	43.4
4. Availing AI (%)	38.5	30.2	25.0	65.8	48.0	56.6
5. Availing health care (%)	42.5	28.7	35.6	65.3	47.3	56.3
6. Animals insured (% to total animals)	17.5	10.0	13.4	25.6	20.3	22.6
7. Attendance in general body (%)	38.3	30.0	27.6	58.3	45.0	50.3

Source: Field study.

Women attend multiple activities in their day to day life. These activities can broadly be divided into household, agriculture, animal husbandry, and small scale industries. Each of these activities can further be bifurcated into various sub-activities. Household work includes cooking food, fetching water, fuel, cleaning house, and utensils washing clothes, baby care and looking after old, and sick, etc. Agriculture includes hired wage labour, or work on own farm. This include preparation of nursery, seedbeds, weeding, transplantation, harvesting, etc. Dairying is the major activity in animal husbandry. Earlier studies indicated that women are responsible for as much 80-85% work associated with dairying and they get trained (informally) since their childhood. SSI includes petty trade (grocery, vegetable vendor, pan shop, etc.), handlooms, handicrafts, goldsmith, pot making, basket weaving, etc.

Table 6.8

Time (hours/day) Allocation of Women among Various Activities in Andhra Pradesh and Karnataka

State	*Household*	*Agriculture*	*Animal husbandry*	*SSI*	*Total*
Andhra Pradesh					
STEP	4.2	3.0	2.7	0.8	10.7
NON-STEP	5.1	3.3	2.0	0.5	10.9
Average	4.7	3.3	2.2	0.5	10.7
Karnataka					
STEP	5.2	3.5	4.0	0.6	13.3
NON-STEP	4.6	4.4	3.0	0.7	12.7
Average	4.8	4.0	3.6	0.7	13.1

Source: Field study.

An analysis of data on allocation of time by these women indicate that women from Karnataka had put in as much as 13.1 hours/day as against 10.7 hours/day in Andhra Pradesh. However, differences between STEP and NON-STEP WDCSs are marginal. One interesting thing that emerges from Table 6.8 is that women of STEP WDCSs are spending relatively more time on animal husbandry, while NON-STEP WDCSs spend more time on agriculture. Thus, dairying helps in providing employment within the house and thus avoid 'going out' which is not considered as status symbol in the rural setting. This also help them avoiding problems associated with 'out side work'. Dairy women of Gujarat spend more time than women of Andhra Pradesh and Karnataka (Rao, 2000). It is mainly due to large volume of milk business and the associated work with it.

Table 6.9

Distribution of Average Income (rupees) from Dairying among Sample Respondents

Land holding (ha)	*Andhra Pradesh*		*Karnataka*	
	STEP	*NON-STEP*	*STEP*	*NON-STEP*
Landless	3082	1355	6675	1675
0.1-1.0	3842	2027	8054	2236
1.1-2.0	4875	2450	9045	3356
2.1-4.0	7080	3068	13089	7035
4.1 and above	9046	3675	16648	8419
Average	5585	2515	10702	4544

Source: Field study.

Table 6.10

Preferred Sex of Additional Children (%)

Opinion	*Andhra Pradesh*			*Karnataka*		
	STEP	*NON-STEP*	*Average*	*STEP*	*NON-STEP*	*Average*
Boy	31.7	38.3	35.0	25.0	33.3	29.2
Girl	13.3	20.0	16.7	11.7	21.7	16.7
Doesn't matter	25.0	16.7	20.8	33.3	16.7	25.0
Up to god	20.0	13.3	16.7	21.7	15.0	18.3
Don't want	10.0	11.7	10.8	8.3	13.3	10.8
Total	100.0	100.0	100.0	100.0	100.0	100.0

Source: Field study.

Income from the sale of milk is paid once a week or fortnightly in the study area. Baring few exceptions its flow is regular and certain. An attempt is made to ascertain the contribution of income from dairying in absolute terms

(Table 6.9). As expected, there are large variations in incomes realized among STEP and NON-STEP WDCSs. Contributing factors for this higher realization are already discussed. The average income/member of STEP WDCSs is more than double than the NON-STEP WDCSs and once again Karnataka maintained its lead over Andhra Pradesh.

Given the socio-economic background in the previous paragraphs, women are asked to give their preference to sex of an additional child. This is solicited because there is a strong desire among women to have a son. A number of reasons are cited for this male biasedness. Not only women themselves, but also in-laws and society's respect to a woman depend on the sex of the children she has. There are instances when women anxiously waited for 6-7 deliveries to have son, circumstances where in-laws and husband ill-treated her for not giving a son, circumstances where women are sent for natal home for not giving sons, etc. Table 6.10 indicated a slight improvement in the attitude of women. Only 1/3rd, on an average, opted for son while surprisingly 17% opted for daughter. As much as 21-25% felt no difference between son and/or daughter. Such improvement in the attitude of women is a good sign for proper sex ratio. These positive changes are mainly attributed to awareness created by WDCSs and involvement of women in a cooperative (WDCS). It is difficult to put a price tag to such a positive contribution but a commendable achievement in deed.

Decision Making Process among Women

In a male dominated society like ours, women take passive role in decision making in different spheres of life (household, agriculture, animal husbandry, small scale industries, etc.). Participation of women in decision making at all levels has special significance, especially in a democratic set up. Decision making is important because the success of an enterprise depends upon how a family takes decisions. The extent of participation in household decision making process could alone be the indicator of woman's status in the household. Their participation in decision making shall explain their control over household activity, education to children, sale/purchase, health, etc. Participation of women in these activities is effected by factors like age, level of education, caste, land holding, and maternal place.

Table 6.11

Factors Affecting Participation in Decision-making among STEP WDCSs of Andhra Pradesh

Sr.No.	*Factor*	*Level of participation*			*Total*
		Low	*Medium*	*High*	
1.	*Age (years)*				
	Up to 21	5 (35.7)	7 (50.0)	2 (14.3)	14 (23.3)
	22-35	8 (32.0)	12 (48.0)	5 (20.0)	25 (41.7)
	36-45	5 (41.7)	4 (33.3)	3 (25.0)	12 (20.0)
	46 and above	4 (44.4)	4 (44.4)	1 (11.2)	9 (15.0)
2.	*Level of education*				
	illiterate	6 (75.0)	2 (25.0)	0 (0.0)	8 (13.3)
	can sign	7 (63.6)	4 (36.4)	0 (0.0)	11 (18.3)
	1-5	5 (22.7)	14 (63.6)	3 (13.7)	22 (36.7)
	6-10	2 (20.0)	4 (40.0)	4 (40.0)	10 (16.7)
	11 and above	0 (0.0)	4 (44.4)	5 (55.6)	9 (15.0)

(Contd.)

Sr.No.	Factor	Level of participation			Total
		Low	*Medium*	*High*	
3.	*Caste*				
	FC	5 (29.4)	6 (35.3)	6 (35.3)	17 (28.3)
	BC	7 (26.9)	15 (57.7)	4 (15.4)	26 (43.4)
	SC/ST	9 (52.9)	7 (41.2)	1 (5.9)	17 (28.3)
4.	*Landholding (ha)*				
	landless	12 (70.6)	5 (29.4)	0 (0.0)	17 (28.3)
	0.1-1.0	12 (60.0)	5 (25.0)	3 (15.0)	20 (33.4)
	1.1-2.0	3 (27.3)	6 (54.5)	2 (18.2)	11 (18.3)
	2.1-4.0	1 (14.3)	4 (57.1)	2 (28.6)	7 (11.7)
	4.1 and above	0 (0.0)	2 (40.0)	3 (60.0)	5 (8.3)
5.	*Maternal place*				
	Urban	2 (9.1)	12 (54.5)	8 (36.4)	22 (36.7)
	Rural	15 (39.5)	19 (50.0)	4 (10.5)	38 (63.3)

Source: Field study.

Careful observation of Tables 6.11 and 6.12 reveals mixed results. Women having the age of less than 35 participated more in decision making process in both the states. There is an inverse relationship between age and level of participation after 35 years. Further, there is a positive association between level of education and level of participation by women among all categories.

Table 6.12

Factors Affecting Participation in Decision-making among NON-STEP WDCSs of Andhra Pradesh

Sr.No.	*Factor*	*Level of participation*			*Total*
		Low	*Medium*	*High*	
1.	*Age (years)*				
	Up to 21	3 (62.5)	0 (37.5)	8 (0.0)	(13.3)
	22-35	5 (41.7)	4 (33.3)	3 (25.0)	12 (20.0)
	36-45	4 (26.7)	8 (53.3)	3 (20.0)	15 (25.0)
	46 and above	12 (48.0)	9 (36.0)	4 (16.0)	25 (41.7)
2.	*Level of education*				
	illiterate	6 (54.5)	5 (45.5)	0 (0.0)	11 (18.3)
	can sign	5 (41.7)	7 (58.3)	0 (0.0)	12 (20.0)
	1-5	7 (29.2)	13 (54.3)	3 (12.5)	24 (40.0)
	6-10	2 (22.2)	4 (44.5)	3 (33.3)	9 (15.0)
	11 and above	0 (0.0)	3 (75.0)	1 (25.0)	4 (6.7)
3.	*Caste*				
	FC	3 (16.7)	10 (55.6)	5 (27.7)	18 (30.0)
	BC	8 (33.3)	12 (50.0)	4 (16.2)	24 (40.0)
	SC/ST	7 (38.9)	8 (44.4)	3 (16.7)	18 (30.0)

(Contd.)

Sr.No.	*Factor*	*Level of participation*			*Total*
		Low	*Medium*	*High*	
4.	*Land holding (ha)*				
	landless	9 (60.0)	5 (33.3)	1 (6.7)	15 (25.0)
	0.1 - 1.0	8 (44.4)	8 (44.4)	2 (11.2)	18 (30.0)
	1.1 - 2.0	3 (25.0)	6 (50.0)	3 (25.0)	12 (20.0)
	2.1 - 4.0	2 (25.0)	5 (62.5)	1 (12.5)	8 (13.3)
	4.1 and above	1 (14.4)	4 (57.1)	2 (28.6)	7 (11.7)
5.	*Maternal place*				
	Urban	4 (26.7)	8 (53.3)	3 (20.0)	15 (25.0)
	Rural	18 (40.0)	22 (48.9)	5 (11.1)	45 (75.0)

Source: Field study.

Table 6.13

Factors Affecting Participation in Decision-Making among STEP WDCSs of Karnataka

Sr. No.	*Factor*	*Level of participation*			*Total*
		Low	*Medium*	*High*	
1.	*Age (years)*				
	Up to 21	7 (46.7)	8 (53.3)	0 (0.0)	15 (25.0)
	22-35	5 (19.2)	9 (34.6)	12 (46.2)	26 (43.4)
	36-45	2 (18.2)	5 (45.4)	4 (36.4)	11 ((18.3)
	46 and above	4 (50.0)	4 (50.0)	0 (0.0)	8 (13.3)

(Contd.)

Sr. No.	Factor	Level of participation			Total
		Low	Medium	High	
2.	*Level of education*				
	illiterate	5	2	0	7
		(71.4)	(28.6)	(0.0)	(11.7)
	can sign	5	4	1	10
		(50.0)	(40.0)	(10.0)	(16.7)
	1-5	4	12	6	22
		(18.2)	(54.5)	(27.3)	(36.7)
	6-10	0	5	6	11
		(0.0)	(45.6)	(54.5)	(18.3)
	11 and above	0	5	5	10
		(0.0)	(50.0)	(50.0)	(16.6)
3.	*Caste*				
	FC	1	6	5	12
		(8.3)	(50.0)	(41.7)	(20.0)
	BC	9	17	6	32
		(28.1)	(53.1)	(18.8)	(53.3)
	SC/ST	6	2	16	18
		(50.0)	(37.5)	(12.2)	(26.7)
4.	*Land holding (ha)*				
	landless	9	10	2	21
		(42.9)	(47.6)	(9.5)	(35.0)
	0.1-1.0	5	10	5	20
		(25.0)	(50.0)	(25.0)	(33.3)
	1.1-2.0	1	5	3	9
		(11.1)	(55.6)	(33.3)	(15.0)
	2.1-4.0	3	4	3	10
		(30.0)	(40.0)	(30.0)	(16.7)
	4.1 and above	0	0	0	0
		(0.0)	(0.0)	(0.0)	(0.0)
5.	*Maternal place*				
	Urban	5	10	10	25
		(20.0)	(40.0)	(40.0)	(41.7)
	Rural	18	11	6	35
		(51.4)	(31.4)	(17.2)	(58.3)

Source: Field study.

A word about education is in order here. School plays a vital role in shaping the destiny of women. School has unique quality or capacity to reduce gap between rich and poor, high and low, and thus paves way for an egalitarian society. Weinberg (1971) observes that 'there is no structure in our society so uniquely equipped to assimilate the poor into mainstream of society as is the school'. The school attempts to assimilate the poor by instilling in all students a similar set of values... Assimilation is also intended by way of providing an access for strata to educational opportunities. Education, particularly formal education, has very significant role to play in accordance to social status of women. It is a major avenue of upward social mobility (Stub, 1975). The findings of the study are in accordance with above observations. Thus, education is found to be an important factor influencing the involvement of women in decision making. Caste-wise participation of women in decision making indicated high level of participation (35.3%) by the women of FCs followed by BCs, and SCs/STs. Only 6% of the SCs/STs women had high level of participation who are mostly educated.

Similarly, size of land holding too had positive influence on decision-making. Higher the size of land holding more is the level of participation. Respondents of large sized land holdings (ha. 4.1 and above) reported high level of participation followed by medium, small, and landless categories. None of the landless women have high level of participation while 60% of the large holdings have high level of participation. Most of these women are educated, have fixed assets on their name, and have exposure to developmental activities, hence high level of participation.

Analysis of data on the basis of maternal place indicated as much as 25-35% are from urban and semi-urban areas. It is assumed that women from urban areas are relatively educated and fear free than their rural counterparts. Interestingly, women whose maternal place is urban/semi-urban areas, had a high level of participation in decision making. Their percentage of high participation in decision making ranged between 25 in NON-STEP WDCSs of Andhra Pradesh to 42 in STEP WDCSs of Karnataka. This high level of participation in decision making could be another reason for better performance of STEP WDCSs compared to their counterparts in Andhra Pradesh and Karnataka.

Thus, women with age between 21-35 having more than eleven years of schooling, belonging to upper castes with larger land holdings and with urban maternal place have high level of participation in decision making process in the study area. These results are, more or less, supported by Dubey, et.al. (1982), Jamal (1989), Kishor, et.al. (1999), Menon (1981), Pandey and Devi (2000), and Singh, et.al. (1991). We have to bear in mind the type of social stratification that exists in rural India. There are several categories of rural women based on religion, caste, education, income, occupation, age, and so on. Hence, a cross sectional study is required to understand the time picture of status of rural women. In order to effectively involve women in decision making process, women have to be empowered first educationally, and in skill formation and upgradation (Giri, 1998). Further, socio-cultural and institutional practices in ownership of property and/or access to land related resources, credit, technology, etc. must be women friendly. Women should also have possibilities of making alternative choices in the paradigms of development.

Impact of WDCSs on Women

This section is divided into two parts: (a) awareness about social organisations, and (b) members perceptions about WDCSs. Participation of human beings in social organisations is their inherent right. The word 'social organisation' is used here to describe vast, complex network of patterned human behavior within a society. Social organisations, if well organised, and directed can be made key instruments of change in rural society in general and rural women in particular (Khan, and Aysha, 1982). They are broadly divided into 'formal' and 'non-formal' organisations. While a formal organisation is a predetermined arrangement of individuals whose interrelated tasks and specialties enable total aggregate to achieve goals, the non-formal organisation is not a predetermined arrangement. Common goal of these two categories of organisations is the progress and prosperity of its members. Social organisations considered in the study are WDCSs, PACSs, PHCs, panchayats, schools, mahila mandals, youth clubs, SHGs, and NGOs. Awareness of the existence and its contribution is a prerequisite for participation. The sources of awareness considered are self, husband, neighbours, officials, and none. The results for all the four categories of WDCSs are presented through Tables 6.14 to 6.17.

Table 6.14

Factors Affecting Participation in Decision-Making among NON- STEP WDCSs of Karnataka

Sr. No.	*Factor*	*Level of participation*			*Total*
		Low	*Medium*	*High*	
1.	*Age (years)*				
	Up to 21	6 (60.0)	2 (20.0)	2 (20.0)	10 (16.7)
	22-35	2 (25.0)	4 (50.0)	2 (25.0)	8 (13.3)
	36-45	5 (21.7)	11 (47.8)	7 (30.4)	23 ((38.3)
	46 and above	3 (15.8)	12 (63.2)	4 (21.0)	19 (31.7)
2.	*Level of education*				
	illiterate	6 (60.0)	3 (30.0)	1 (10.0)	10 (16.7)
	can sign	4 (36.4)	4 (36.4)	3 (27.2)	11 (18.3)
	1-5	6 (25.0)	13 (54.2)	5 (20.8)	24 (40.0)
	6-10	2 (22.2)	4 (44.4)	3 (33.3)	9 (15.0)
	11 and above	1 (16.7)	2 (33.3)	3 (50.0)	6 (10.0)

(Contd.)

Sr. No.	*Factor*	*Level of participation*			*Total*
		Low	*Medium*	*High*	
3.	*Caste*				
	FC	2 (14.4)	6 (42.8)	6 (42.8)	14 (23.3)
	BC	10 (33.3)	12 (40.0)	8 (26.7)	30 (50.0)
	SC/ST	9 (56.3)	4 (25.0)	3 (18.7)	16 (26.7)
4.	*Land holding (ha)*				
	Landless	8 (53.3)	6 (40.0)	1 (6.7)	15 (25.0)
	0.1-1.0	5 (26.3)	9 (47.4)	5 (26.3)	19 (31.7)
	1.1-2.0	3 (25.0)	6 (50.0)	3 (25.0)	12 (20.0)
	2.1-4.0	1 (12.5)	4 (50.0)	3 (37.5)	8 (13.3)
	4.1 and above	1 (16.7)	2 (33.3)	3 (50.0)	6 (10.0)
5.	*Maternal place*				
	Urban	3 (15.8)	11 (57.9)	5 (26.3)	19 (31.7)
	Rural	15 (36.6)	20 (48.8)	6 (14.6)	41 (68.3)

Source: Field study.

Table 6.15

Sources of Awareness about Village Organisations among STEP WDCSs of Andhra Pradesh

Organisation	*Self*	*Husband*	*Neighbours*	*Officials*	*None*	*Total*
1. WDCSs	22 (36.7)	15 (25.0)	18 (30.0)	5 (8.3)	0 (0.0)	60 (100.0)
2. PACSs	8 (13.3)	24 (40.0)	13 (21.7)	3 (5.0)	12 (20.0)	60 (100.0)

(Contd.)

Organisation	Self	Husband	Neighbours	Officials	None	Total
3. PHCs	10 (16.7)	15 (25.0)	19 (31.7)	11 (18.3)	5 (8.3)	60 (100.0)
4. Panchayats	14 (23.3)	20 (33.4)	17 (28.3)	7 (11.7)	2 (3.3)	60 (100.0)
5. Schools	21 (35.0)	9 (15.0)	18 (30.0)	3 (5.0)	9 (15.0)	60 (100.0)
6. Mahila Mandals	28 (46.7)	5 (8.3)	19 (31.7)	2 (3.3)	6 (10.0)	60 (100.0)
7. Youth clubs	16 (26.7)	10 (16.7)	15 (25.0)	0 (0.0)	19 (31.7)	60 (100.0)
8. SHGs	3 (5.0)	5 (8.3)	32 (53.3)	14 (23.3)	6 (10.0)	60 (100.0)
9. NGOs	9 (15.0)	11 (18.3)	12 (20.0)	8 (13.4)	20 (33.3)	60 (100.0)

Source: Field study.

Table 6.16

Sources of Awareness about Village Organisations among NON-STEP WDCSs of Andhra Pradesh

Organisation	Self	Husband	Neighbours	Officials	None	Total
1. WDCSs	7 (11.7)	24 (40.0)	22 (36.6)	7 (11.7)	0 (0.0)	60 (100.0)
2. PACSs	8 (13.3)	30 (50.0)	10 (16.7)	2 (3.3)	10 (16.7)	60 (100.0)
3. PHCs	9 (15.0)	13 (21.7)	20 (33.3)	10 (16.7)	8 (13.3)	60 (100.0)
4. Panchayats	9 (15.0)	18 (30.0)	22 (36.6)	4 (6.7)	7 (11.7)	60 (100.0)
5. Schools	14 (23.3)	10 (16.7)	18 (30.0)	2 (3.3)	16 (26.7)	60 (100.0)
6. Mahila Mandals	15 (25.0)	5 (8.3)	25 (41.7)	3 (5.0)	12 (20.0)	60 (100.0)

(Contd.)

Organisation	*Self*	*Husband*	*Neighbours*	*Officials*	*None*	*Total*
7. Youth clubs	6 (10.0)	10 (16.7)	20 (33.3)	7 (11.7)	17 (28.3)	60 (100.0)
8. SHGs	3 (5.0)	10 (16.7)	18 (30.0)	10 (16.7)	19 (31.6)	60 (100.0)
9. NGOs	5 (8.3)	8 (13.3)	15 (25.0)	5 (8.3)	27 (45.0)	60 (100.0)

Source: Field study.

Table 6.17

Sources of Awareness about Village Organisations among STEP WDCSs of Karnataka

Organisation	*Self*	*Husband*	*Neighbours*	*Officials*	*None*	*Total*
1. WDCSs	29 (48.3)	12 (20.0)	15 (25.0)	4 (6.7)	0 (0.0)	60 (100.0)
2. PACSs	6 (10.0)	20 (33.3)	10 (16.7)	14 (23.3)	10 (16.7)	60 (100.0)
3. PHCs	25 (41.7)	13 (21.7)	22 (36.6)	6 (10.0)	3 (5.0)	60 (100.0)
4. Panchayats	16 (26.7)	15 (25.0)	19 (31.6)	8 (13.4)	2 (3.3)	60 (100.0)
5. Schools	26 (43.3)	4 (6.6)	16 (26.7)	7 (11.7)	7 (11.7)	60 (100.0)
6. Mahila Mandals	30 (50.0)	2 (3.3)	15 (25.0)	9 (15.0)	4 (6.7)	60 (100.0)
7. Youth clubs	15 (25.0)	8 (13.3)	20 (33.4)	2 (3.3)	15 (25.0)	60 (100.0)
8. SHGs	12 (20.0)	10 (16.7)	21 (35.0)	12 (20.0)	5 (8.3)	60 (100.0)
9. NGOs	4 (6.6)	10 (16.7)	24 (40.0)	7 (11.7)	15 (25.0)	60 (100.0)

Source: Field study.

Table 6.18
Sources of Awareness about Village Organisations among NON-STEP WDCSs of Karnataka

Organisation	*Self*	*Husband*	*Neighbours*	*Officials*	*None*	*Total*
1. WDCSs	18 (30.0)	8 (13.3)	25 (41.7)	9 (15.0)	0 (0.0)	60 (100.0)
2. PACSs	7 (11.7)	15 (25.0)	18 (30.0)	5 (8.3)	15 (25.0)	60 (100.0)
3. PHCs	15 (25.0)	12 (20.0)	19 (31.7)	6 (10.0)	8 (13.3)	60 (100.0)
4. Panchayats	19 (31.7)	17 (28.3)	15 (25.0)	4 (6.7)	5 (8.3)	60 (100.0)
5. Schools	25 (41.7)	7 (11.7)	14 (23.3)	8 (13.3)	6 (10.0)	60 (100.0)
6. Mahila Mandals	31 (51.7)	7 (11.7)	16 (26.6)	2 (3.3)	4 (6.7)	60 (100.0)
7. Youth clubs	12 (20.0)	8 (13.3)	25 (41.7)	2 (3.3)	13 (21.7)	60 (100.0)
8. SHGs	15 (25.0)	10 (16.7)	28 (46.7)	3 (5.0)	4 (6.6)	60 (100.0)
9. NGOs	12 (20.0)	14 (23.3)	10 (16.7)	12 (20.0)	14 (23.3)	60 (100.0)

Source: Field study.

The extent of awareness among respondents about various organisations varied widely. There is cent percent awareness about WDCSs among all the members studied. Next in the order is panchayats, schools, and PHCs. All the above four organisations are of vital importance in the village and more so for women. Due to recent 73rd and 74th amendments to our constitution, women are given 33% reservation in all these organisations that brought a sea change in the women. WDCSs have also been making efforts to bring awareness in women. As regards sources of awareness, it is mostly self, husband, and neighbours. Government officials have not played their role effectively in creating awareness among respondents. May be they thought that 'other' social organisations would take care of creating awareness or they are already over burdened with their routine work.

Table 6.19

Advantage of Village Organisations for Development of Women (STEP WDCSs of Andhra Pradesh)

Organisation	*Very useful*	*Useful*	*Not useful*	*No idea*	*Total*
1. WDCSs	20 (33.3)	28 (46.7)	4 (6.7)	8 (13.3)	60 (100.0)
2. PACSs	17 (28.3)	22 (36.7)	6 (10.0)	15 (25.0)	60 (100.0)
3. PHCs	14 (23.3)	29 (48.4)	5 (8.3)	12 (20.0)	60 (100.0)
4. Panchayats	11 (18.3)	30 (50.0)	9 (15.0)	10 (16.7)	60 (100.0)
5. Schools	23 (38.3)	28 (46.7)	0 (0.0)	9 (15.0)	60 (100.0)
6. Mahila Mandals	15 (25.0)	35 (58.3)	2 (3.3)	8 (13.3)	60 (100.0)
7. Youth clubs	11 (18.3)	20 (33.4)	15 (25.0)	14 (23.3)	60 (100.0)
8. SHGs	18 (30.0)	23 (38.3)	9 (15.0)	10 (16.7)	60 (100.0)
9. NGOs	14 (23.3)	22 (36.7)	0 (0.0)	24 (40.0)	60 (100.0)

Source: Field study.

As expected, very low percentage of women are aware of PACSs which is locally known as 'bank'. It is mainly due to its special feature of dealing with landed category which is mostly owned by men. Interestingly, husbands played major role in bringing awareness about PHCs, panchayats, and schools. This observation holds true across all four categories of WDCSs studied. Women themselves are aware of mahila mandals and neighbours too contributed in this regard.

Table 6.20

Advantage of Village Organisations for Development of Women (NON-STEP WDCSs of Andhra Pradesh)

Organisation	*Very useful*	*Useful*	*Not useful*	*No idea*	*Total*
1. WDCSs	10 (16.7)	28 (46.7)	12 (20.0)	10 (16.7)	60 (100.0)
2. PACSs	15 (25.0)	18 (30.0)	8 (13.3)	19 (31.7)	60 (100.0)
3. PHCs	12 (20.0)	21 (35.0)	9 (15.0)	18 (30.0)	60 (100.0)
4. Panchayats	8 (13.3)	25 (41.7)	12 (20.0)	15 (25.0)	60 (100.0)
5. Schools	20 (33.3)	24 (40.0)	5 (8.3)	11 (18.3)	60 (100.0)
6. Mahila Mandals	15 (25.0)	25 (41.7)	6 (10.0)	14 (23.3)	60 (100.0)
7. Youth clubs	12 (20.0)	22 (36.7)	6 (10.0)	20 (33.3)	60 (100.0)
8. SHGs	15 (25.0)	20 (33.3)	13 (21.7)	12 (20.0)	60 (100.0)
9. NGOs	10 (16.7)	18 (30.0)	12 (20.0)	20 (33.3)	60 (100.0)

Source: Field study.

Large proportion of respondents from Karnataka came to know about these organisations on their own than in Andhra Pradesh. Awareness about SHGs and NGOs is abysmal in Andhra Pradesh while it is picking up in Karnataka. These two organisations are relatively new and would take some more time to familiarize themselves with rural women. Further, outsiders hesitate to approach women due to social restrictions and taboos imposed on such meetings. However, there is considerable change in the villages covered and women are freely, to a large extend, talking to outsiders and sharing their experiences and problems. This is made possible through positive change in the mindsets of both women and men and organisations like WDCSs are responsible for this.

Table 6.21

Advantage of Village Organisations for Development of Women (STEP WDCSs of Karnataka)

Organisation	*Very useful*	*Useful*	*Not useful*	*No idea*	*Total*
1. WDCSs	28 (46.7)	30 (50.0)	2 (3.3)	0 (0.0)	60 (100.0)
2. PACSs	15 (25.0)	28 (46.7)	8 (13.3)	9 (15.0)	60 (100.0)
3. PHCs	16 (26.7)	32 (53.3)	9 (15.0)	3 (5.0)	60 (100.0)
4. Panchayats	14 (23.3)	29 (48.3)	5 (8.3)	12 (20.0)	60 (100.0)
5. Schools	19 (31.7)	31 (51.7)	0 (0.0)	10 (16.7)	60 (100.0)
6. Mahila Mandals	21 (35.0)	32 (53.3)	4 (6.7)	3 (5.0)	60 (100.0)
7. Youth clubs	15 (25.0)	22 (36.7)	13 (21.6)	10 (16.7)	60 (100.0)
8. SHGs	17 (28.3)	25 (41.7)	9 (15.0)	9 (15.0)	60 (100.0)
9. NGOs	16 (26.7)	26 (43.3)	8 (13.3)	10 (16.7)	60 (100.0)

Source: Field study.

The respondents are asked to express their opinions regarding advantages of these organisations for development of women and results are presented in Tables 6.18 to 6.21. Their contribution is measured as 'very useful', 'useful', 'not useful', and 'no idea'. There are wide variations in the responses given by members across states. They differed from state to state and within the state. Relatively higher percentages of women from STEP WDCSs of Andhra Pradesh reported contribution of these organisations as very useful compared to NON-STEP WDCSs of Andhra Pradesh. Among all the social organisations considered, schools, WDCSs and NGOs turned out to be very useful in STEP WDCSs of Andhra Pradesh while schools, mahila mandals, SHGs, and PHCs got this rating in NON-STEP WDCSs of Andhra Pradesh. The least number expressing dismal or pessimistic shade of opinion is in the case of NGOs in Andhra Pradesh. On the whole, majority of members expressed either 'very useful', or 'useful' and put together 60-70% of respondents stated that almost all organisations studied have been contributing for the development of women.

Table 6.22

Advantage of Village Organisations for Development of Women (NON-STEP WDCSs of Karnataka)

Organisation	*Very useful*	*Useful*	*Not Useful*	*No idea*	*Total*
1. WDCSs	13 (21.7)	32 (53.3)	7 (11.7)	8 (13.3)	60 (100.0)
2. PACSs	18 (30.0)	23 (38.3)	10 (16.7)	9 (15.0)	60 (100.0)
3. PHCs	15 (25.0)	28 (46.6)	10 (16.7)	7 (11.7)	60 (100.0)
4. Panchayats	10 (16.7)	29 (48.3)	12 (20.0)	9 (15.0)	60 (100.0)
5. Schools	22 (36.7)	29 (48.3)	0 (0.0)	9 (15.0)	60 (100.0)
6. Mahila Mandals	20 (33.3)	24 (40.0)	5 (8.3)	11 (18.3)	60 (100.0)
7. Youth clubs	17 (28.3)	20 (33.3)	5 (8.3)	18 (30.0)	60 (100.0)
8. SHGs	15 (25.0)	28 (46.6)	7 (11.7)	10 (16.7)	60 (100.0)
9. NGOs	8 (13.3)	24 (40.0)	10 (16.7)	18 (30.0)	60 (100.0)

Source: Field study.

The situation is much better in Karnataka. As much as 47% of the members of STEP WDCSs mentioned that WDCSs are 'very useful' as against 22% in NON-STEP WDCSs. Only 3% of STEP WDCSs informed that WDCSs are not useful. Mahila mandals and schools once again received appreciation of women from both STEP and NON-STEP areas. Attitude towards SHGs and NGOs is much better in Karnataka. On the whole, those who have 'no idea' about the contribution of organisations constituted a small number. In general, it could be concluded that those who appreciated the usefulness ('very useful' and 'useful') of the organisations account for a large number than those who expressed their ignorance.

Table 6.23

Members' Perceptions about Impact of WDCS on their Lives (Andhra Pradesh)

Indicator	*Improved*		*No change*		*Decreased*		*Total*	
	STEP	*NON-STEP*	*STEP*	*NON-STEP*	*STEP*	*NON-STEP*	*STEP*	*NON-STEP*
Intake of food	24 (40.0)	17 (28.3)	36 (60.0)	43 (71.7)	0 (0.0)	0 (0.0)	60 (100.0)	60 (100.0)
Health condition	30 (50.0)	19 (31.7)	29 (48.3)	39 (65.0)	1 (1.7)	2 (3.3)	60 (100.0)	60 (100.0)
Better clothing	35 (58.3)	22 (36.7)	25 (41.7)	38 (63.3)	0 (0.0)	0 (0.0)	60 (100.0)	60 (100.0)
Enhanced savings	37 (61.7)	25 (41.7)	21 (35.0)	33 (55.0)	2 (3.3)	2 (3.3)	60 (100.0)	60 (100.0)
Participation in decision making	25 (41.7)	18 (30.0)	35 (58.3)	41 (68.3)	0 (0.0)	1 (1.7)	60 (100.0)	60 (100.0)
Awareness	32 (53.3)	18 (30.0)	28 (46.7)	42 (70.0)	0 (0.0)	0 (0.0)	60 (100.0)	60 (100.0)

Note : Figures in parentheses are percentages to row totals.

Source: Field study.

While the earlier discussion covered the advantages of various social organisations, an attempt is made here to specially inquire about the impact of WDCSs on their lives. Impact is measured for indicators like intake of food, health condition, better clothing, enhanced savings, participation in decision making, and creating awareness. Level of impact is measured as 'improved', 'no change' and, 'decreased' and the results for Andhra Pradesh and Karnataka are presented respectively in Tables 6.22 and 6.23. As much as 40-62% of the respondents of STEP societies mentioned that the level of impact is 'improved' while it ranged between 27-42% in NON-STEP societies. Enhanced savings (improved) got the highest percentage in STEP societies while in take of food (no change) got the maximum percentage in NON-STEP societies. Few women reported decrease in the indicators considered. These abnormalities are covered, to some extent, in individual case studies.

Table 6.24

Members' Perceptions about Impact of WDCS on their Lives (Karnataka)

Indicator	*Improved*		*No change*		*Decreased*		*Total*	
	STEP	*NON-STEP*	*STEP*	*NON-STEP*	*STEP*	*NON-STEP*	*STEP*	*NON-STEP*
Intake of food	53 (88.3)	40 (66.7)	7 (11.7)	20 (33.3)	0 (0.0)	0 (0.0)	60 (100.0)	60 (100.0)
Health condition	48 (80.0)	37 (61.7)	12 (20.0)	22 (35.7)	0 (0.0)	1 (1.6)	60 (100.0)	60 (100.0)
Better clothing	50 (83.3)	42 (70.0)	10 (16.7)	18 (30.0)	0 (0.0)	0 (0.0)	60 (100.0)	60 (100.0)
Enhanced saving	50 (83.3)	35 (58.3)	10 (16.7)	24 (40.0)	0 (0.0)	1 (0.7)	60 (100.0)	60 (100.0)
Participation in decision making	52 (86.7)	28 (46.7)	8 (13.3)	32 (53.3)	0 (0.0)	0 (0.0)	60 (100.0)	60 (100.0)
Awareness	54 (30.0)	31 (51.7)	6 (10.0)	29 (48.3)	0 (0.0)	0 (0.0)	60 (100.0)	60 (100.0)

Note : Figures in parentheses are percentages to row totals.

Source: Field study.

Relatively better results are reported by the women respondents from Karnataka. More than 80% of the respondents of STEP societies mentioned substantial improvement in the indicators considered and only two women, across all indicators, mentioned decrease. The percentage of respondents reporting 'improved' condition slightly declined in NON-STEP societies, but it is more than 50% for the all indicators.

Thus, WDCSs have contributed substantially for the improvement in the selected indicators in both the states, however, it is more so in the case of STEP societies. These positive, observable, and non-observable changes would go a long way in empowering women.

Summary

An overview of respondents revealed that, on the whole, a quarter of women members belong to landless category in the both states, third of them are marginal farmers and about 50-55% of them maintained one animal. Caste-wise, FCs and SCs/STs each constituted 30% followed by BCs in the study area. Majority of respondents are literate. As regards involvement of members in society's activities, higher percentages of involvement is reported from STEP WDCSs of Karnataka than their counterparts of the study. Data on allocation of time by the respondents indicated that women from Karnataka had put in as much as 13.1 hours/day as against 10.7 hours/day in Andhra Pradesh. Women of STEP WDCSs are spending more time on animal husbandry, while NON-STEP WDCSs spend more time on agriculture. There are large variations in incomes realized among STEP and NON-STEP WDCSs.

Women with age between 21-35, having more than eleven years of schooling, belonging to upper castes, with larger land holdings, and with urban maternal place have high level of participation in decision making. Major sources of awareness about social organisations are self, husband, and neighbours. Government officials have not played their role effectively in creating awareness about organisations among respondents. Those who appreciated the usefulness of the organisations account for a large chunk than those who expressed their ignorance. WDCSs have contributed substantially for the improvement in intake of food, health condition, better clothing, enhanced savings, participation in decision making, and creating awareness.

Chapter 7
Empowerment Scores

This chapter is aimed at constructing and comparing empowerment scores for the respondents of STEP and NON-STEP WDCSs separately.

Women's empowerment has recently gained considerable importance as an area of policy intervention in most part of the world. Governments have recognised the benefits of empowerment which can be achieved through effective participation of women. It is a term often used in development work, but rarely defined. In a conventional sense, empowerment is bring people who are outside the decision making process into it (Rowlands, 1997). It puts a strong emphasis on participation in political structures and formal decision making, and on the ability to obtain an income that enables participation in economic decision making.

When viewed from the print of 'power to' and 'power with', empowerment is concerned with process by which people become aware of their own interests and how those relate to interests of others in order both to participate from a position of greater strength in decision making and actually to influence such decision. From a feminist perspective, empowerment is more than participation in decision making. It also includes, the process that lead people to perceive themselves as able and entitled to make decision. It involves giving scope to full range of human abilities and potential. Empowerment must involve undoing negative social construction, so that people come to see themselves as having the capacity and right to act and influence decisions (Rowlands, 1997).

According to Moser (1989), empowerment is the capacity of women to increase their own self-reliance and internal strength. This is identified as the right to determine choices in life and to influence the direction of change through the ability to gain control over material and non-material resources. In the words of Clutterbuck and Stuart (1992), we need not 'empower women' but 'power women' .

As mentioned in Chapter 1, there are very few studies which measured empowerment. Hashemi (1996) developed five indicators to measure women's empowerment: mobility, economic security, ability to make larger purchases, relative freedom from domination within the family, and political and legal awareness, and involvement in political campaigning and protests. With this in mind, an attempt is made in the following sections to measure empowerment of women respondents.

Members' Perception about Empowerment

Respondents of the study are asked to convey their perception about empowerment (Table 7.1). In all, respondents cited seven meanings for empowerment: awareness, education, independent, self-reliance, self-confidence, to stand on own legs, and having cash/property. Of the seven mentioned above, as much as 23% of the respondents from Andhra Pradesh mentioned awareness as empowerment while same perception got 27% in Karnataka. Next in the order is education, independent and self-reliance. Interestingly, very few respondents mentioned that empowerment means 'having cash and property'. Thus, more than 20% of women felt that awareness is necessary condition to attain empowerment.

Having mentioned what is empowerment to them, they also expressed their level of empowerment due to WDCS (Table 7.2). As expected, 30% of the respondents of STEP WDCSs have indicated that they are fully empowered while it is as low as 3.3% in NON-STEP WDCSs of Andhra Pradesh. On the other hand, 75% of the respondents of NON-STEP WDCSs of Andhra Pradesh fall in the category of either 'not at all' empowered or 'no opinion' about it. In contrast to this finding, only 32% of respondents of STEP WDCSs of Karnataka have expressed either 'not at all' empowered or 'no opinion'. The other two categories (STEP WDCSs of Andhra Pradesh and NON-STEP WDCSs of Karnataka) fall in between the two. Thus, respondents of STEP WDCSs of Karnataka are better off in terms of empowerment.

Table 7.1

Members' Perception about Empowerment

Perception	*Andhra Pradesh*			*Karnataka*		
	STEP	*NON-STEP*	*Average*	*STEP*	*NON-STEP*	*Average*
1. Awareness	16 (26.6)	12 (20.0)	28 (23.3)	18 (30.0)	14 (23.0)	32 (26.7)
2. Education	12 (20.0)	12 (20.0)	24 (20.0)	12 (20.0)	13 (21.7)	25 (20.8)
3. Independent	9 (15.0)	10 (16.7)	19 (15.8)	9 (15.0)	11 (18.3)	20 (16.7)
4. Self-reliance	7 (11.7)	9 (15.0)	16 (13.3)	8 (13.3)	9 (15.0)	17 (14.2)
5. Self-confidence	6 (10.0)	8 (13.3)	14 (11.7)	7 (11.7)	6 (10.0)	13 (10.8)
6. To stand on own legs	6 (10.0)	5 (8.3)	11 (9.2)	3 (5.0)	5 (8.3)	8 (6.6)
7. Having cash/ property	4 (6.7)	4 (6.7)	8 (6.7)	3 (5.0)	2 (3.3)	5 (4.2)
Total	60 (100.0)	60 (100.0)	120 (100.0)	60 (100.0)	60 (100.0)	120 (100.0)

Source: Field study.

Table 7.2

Members' Opinion about Their Level of Empowerment Due to Membership in WDCS

Level of empowerment	*Andhra Pradesh*		*Karnataka*	
	STEP	NON-STEP	STEP	NON-STEP
Fully	4 (6.7)	2 (3.3)	18 (30.0)	5 (8.3)
To some extent	15 (25.0)	10 (16.7)	23 (38.3)	18 (30.0)
Not at all	29 (48.3)	33 (55.0)	12 (20.0)	27 (45.0)
No opinion	12 (20.0)	15 (25.0)	7 (11.7)	10 (16.7)
Total	60 (100.0)	60 (100.0)	60 (100.0)	60 (100.0)

Source: Field study.

Empowerment Scores

Based on review of literature on empowerment, discussions with officials connected with implementation of women development programmes, and experts from the field of extension education, 24 empowerment variables are identified (Table 7.3). Each variable is given a maximum score of 3 and minimum of 1. Depending upon the nature of variable, they are given 1, 2 and 3 or 1 or 3. Variables 1-6 are coded as 3 if 'women alone' took decision, 2 if 'women and husbands' took decision, and 1 if 'husband alone' took decision. Similarly, variables 7-22 involved 'yes' or 'no' and 3 is assigned if the answer is 'yes', and 1 if the answer is 'no'. Variables 23-24 too expected 'yes' or 'no' answer but score 1 is assigned if the answer is 'yes', and 3 for 'no'. Variables concerning WDCSs are 1-11, and variables 12-24 are general in nature. The total empowerment score ranged between 24 and 72. Mean scores, standard deviations and 't' values for differences in two mean scores (STEP and NON-STEP areas) for Andhra Pradesh is presented in Table 7.4. An observation of Table 7.4 reveals that

(a) average mean scores, for all the variables considered, are higher for respondents of STEP area, (b) spread of observations from the mean is less in the STEP area, and (c) nine out of 24 variables considered are statistically significant. These findings once again confirms the higher level of awareness and maturity among STEP respondents compared to respondents of NON-STEP WDCSs. Highest average mean score of 2.43 is obtained out of 3 for the variable 'leadership development programmes for women help building confidence'. This finding reaffirms the earlier observation that STEP programme has been contributing successfully in imparting training to its members. Training component is continuous and about 1/3rd of the programme funds are devoted for this purpose under STEP. The situation is different in NON-STEP WDCSs. There is hardly any training component, and members are left to fend themselves to organise the WDCSs. Discussions with officials of the unions revealed that no such funds are available for NON-STEP WDCSs and hence those members were left out of the training calendar.

Table 7.3

Coding of Variables Indicating Women Empowerment

Sl. No.	*Empowerment variable*	*Decision*			*Response*	
		Women	*Both*	*Men*	*Yes*	*No*
1.	Owning animals	3	2	1		
2.	Receipt of milk payment	3	2	1		
3.	Decision taking on AI	3	2	1		
4.	Decision taking on vaccinating animals	3	2	1		
5.	Right to use money earned from milk sales	3	2	1		
6.	Who decide on sale/purchase of animals	3	2	1		
7.	Do you think that your status (your ideas valued) has increased in the house due to membership in society			3	1	

(Contd.)

Sl. No.	*Empowerment variable*	*Decision Women*	*Decision Both*	*Decision Men*	*Response Yes*	*Response No*
8.	Do you think that your status (your ideas valued) has increased in the village due to membership in society				3	1
9.	Do you participate in the AGM regularly				3	1
10.	Are you on the managing committee of the society				3	1
11.	Do you visit the society regularly				3	1
12.	Do you have a saving account in the bank				3	1
13.	Can you decide on the number of children you bear				3	1
14.	Will you give equal education to boys and girls				3	1
15.	Will you treat boys and girls equally (food/clothing/health care/affection)				3	1
16.	Does a daughter have right to decide when to marry				3	1
17.	Does your daughter has right to whom to marry				3	1
18.	Do you think that women should get equal wages for similar work they perform				3	1
19.	Do you think that women are competitive enough to manage a cooperative				3	1
20.	Does women and men display similar leadership traits				3	1
21.	Leadership development programmes for women help building confidence				3	1
22.	Can you exercise vote without consulting husband				3	1
23.	Do you need to take permission to join local women's organisation (mahila mandal)				1	3
24.	Do you need to take permission to attend training program to be conducted outside your village				1	3

Source: Constructed by the author.

Table 7.4

Differences in Empowerment of Women in STEP and NON-STEP WDCSs of Andhra Pradesh

Sl. No.	Indicator	STEP Mean	STEP SD	NON-STEP Mean	NON-STEP SD	't' value
1.	Owning milch animals	2.07	0.53	1.73	0.65	1.85**
2.	Milk payment receipt	1.90	0.75	1.65	0.82	2.23**
3.	Decision on AI	2.03	0.95	1.77	0.90	3.53*
4.	Decision on vaccination	1.62	0.85	1.48	0.88	0.98
5.	Right to use money	1.92	0.66	1.58	0.75	2.75*
6.	Decision on sale/purchase of milch animals	1.82	0.82	1.52	0.88	1.80**
7.	Status in house	2.27	0.53	1.67	0.59	3.23*
8.	Status in village	1.63	0.77	1.37	0.85	1.25
9.	Participation in AGM	1.77	0.58	1.60	0.62	1.01
10.	Member of managing committee	1.50	0.92	1.50	0.98	0.00
11.	Regular visits to WDCS	1.83	1.00	1.47	1.03	1.95**
12.	Status of savings account	1.77	0.75	1.40	0.65	1.43
13.	Right to decide child baring	1.50	0.80	1.33	0.82	0.98
14.	Equal education to boys and girls	1.77	0.72	1.47	0.75	1.25
15.	Equal treatment to boys and girls	1.70	0.68	1.40	0.69	1.11
16.	Daughter's right to marry a person of her choice	1.47	0.70	1.27	0.72	1.27
17.	Daughter's right to timing of marriage	1.47	0.70	1.27	0.72	0.95
18.	Equal wages to women	2.20	0.42	2.00	0.53	1.05
19.	Can women manage a WDCS	2.03	0.35	1.75	0.42	1.97**
20.	Women and men have similar leadership traits	1.83	0.58	1.50	0.60	1.72

(Contd.)

Sl. No.	Indicator	STEP Mean	STEP SD	NON-STEP Mean	NON-STEP SD	't' value
21.	Leadership development programmes for women help building confidence	2.43	0.22	2.00	0.30	2.05**
22.	Can you exercise vote without consulting husband	1.70	0.67	1.40	0.72	1.52
23.	Permission for joining mahila mandal	1.73	0.75	1.60	0.70	1.02
24.	Permission to training program to be conducted outside village	1.67	0.72	1.57	0.65	0.75

** Significant at 5%
* Significant at 1%
Source: Calculated by the author.

The results obtained for the respondents of Karnataka are still encouraging and are as expected (Table 7.5). Here 18 out of 24 variables considered are statistically significant thereby indicating the impact of STEP on its respondents vis-a-via respondents of NON-STEP WDCSs. Highest score of 2.83 is obtained for the variable 'improvement in the status of respondents in their house'. 'Leadership development programmes for women help building confidence' got highest average score (2.50) in NON-STEP WDCSs. This observation stresses the importance of training programmes and the need for arranging such programmes on a priority basis.

Table 7.5

Differences in Empowerment of Women in STEP and NON-STEP WDCSs of Karnataka

Sl. No.	Indicator	STEP Mean	STEP SD	NON-STEP Mean	NON-STEP SD	't' value
1.	Owning milch animals	2.33	0.25	2.23	0.38	0.95
2.	Milk payment receipt	2.25	0.14	1.97	0.56	2.89*
3.	Decision on AI	2.10	0.22	1.93	0.45	2.05**

(Contd.)

Sl. No.	Indicator	STEP Mean	STEP SD	NON-STEP Mean	NON-STEP SD	't' value
4.	Decision on vaccination	1.93	0.35	1.68	0.75	2.45*
5.	Right to use money	2.23	0.25	1.83	0.49	3.86*
6.	Decision on sale/purchase of milch animals	2.11	0.56	2.05	0.75	1.72
7.	Status in house	2.83	0.30	2.40	0.54	4.78*
8.	Status in village	1.93	0.20	1.67	0.63	6.43*
9.	Participation in AGM	2.17	0.15	1.90	0.45	3.61*
10.	Member of managing committee	1.50	1.00	1.50	1.00	0.00
11.	Regular visits to WDCS	2.27	0.24	2.00	0.67	3.78*
12.	Status of savings account	2.40	0.40	1.87	0.85	4.65*
13.	Right to decide child baring	1.73	0.37	1.67	0.62	1.25
14.	Equal education to boys and girls	2.07	0.42	1.90	0.75	1.95**
15.	Equal treatment to boys and girls	2.07	0.35	1.83	0.82	2.00**
16.	Daughter's right to marry a person of her choice	2.00	0.37	1.57	0.63	4.78*
17.	Daughter's right to timing of marriage	2.00	0.35	1.57	0.68	5.75*
18.	Equal wages to women	2.50	0.34	2.33	0.54	1.54
19.	Can women manage a WDCS	2.47	0.50	2.17	0.82	2.75*
20.	Women and men have similar leadership traits	2.30	0.35	1.90	0.55	2.76*
21.	Leadership development programmes for women help building confidence	2.77	0.54	2.50	0.76	1.65
22.	Can you exercise vote without consulting husband	2.33	0.32	1.90	0.54	3.07*
23.	Permission for joining mahila mandal	2.50	0.50	2.00	0.79	4.75*
24.	Permission to training program to be conducted outside village	2.63	0.44	2.07	0.87	5.89*

** Significant at 5%

* Significant at 1%

Source: Calculated by the author.

Table 7.6

Average Minimum, and Maximum Scores Obtained by Sample Respondents

State	*Average*	*Minimum*	*Maximum*
Andhra Pradesh			
STEP	46.94	30.0	64.0
NON-STEP	37.30	28.0	40.0
Karnataka			
STEP	53.62	35.0	67.0
NON-STEP	43.95	30.0	56.0

Source: Calculated by the author.

Score of all the 24 above variables are summed up and minimum and maximum scores obtained by sample respondents are presented in Table 7.6. Average score is the highest (53.62) for STEP WDCSs of Karnataka followed by WDCSs of Andhra Pradesh (46.94), 43.95 for NON-STEP WDCSs of Karnataka, and 37.30 for NON-STEP WDCSs of Andhra Pradesh. Thus, respondents of STEP WDCSs of Karnataka obtained an average score of 53.62 with a range of 35.0 to 67.0. Similarly, respondents of STEP area in Andhra Pradesh obtained an average score of 46.94 with a range of 30.0 to 64.0.

It is to be mentioned here that the concept of empowerment score/index is much of wider and richer than a set of indicators. Such scores are useful in facing attention and simplifying problems. These scores have considerable political appeal. They have stronger impact on mind and draw public attention more powerfully than a long list of indicators combined with qualitative discussions.

A Word of Caution

When measured through above variables a woman may be personally empowered. However, if she continuous to hold full responsibility for household chores followed by responsibilities in agriculture, animal husbandry, and small scale industries, empowerment has increased her burden. In some cases this enables the husband to take up even less responsibilities than before. In essence, empowerment should enable her to share the roles/responsibilities on equal terms with men folk.

Summary

According to respondents, empowerment means awareness, education, being independent, self-reliance, self-confidence, to stand on own legs, and having cash/property. Of the seven indicators mentioned above, as many as 1/4th of respondents, from both Andhra Pradesh and Karnataka, mentioned that 'awareness' as empowerment. Similarly 1/3rd of the respondents of STEP WDCSs indicated that they are 'fully'/'to some extent' empowered while only 12% of respondents of NON-STEP WDCSs from Andhra Pradesh belong to that category. In all 24 empowerment variables are identified and depending upon the nature of variables are given scores as 1, 2, and 3 or 1 or 3. Thus, the total empowerment score ranged between 24 and 72. Average mean scores, for all the variables considered, are higher for respondents of STEP WDCSs and spread of observations from the mean is less. Average score is the highest (53.62) for STEP WDCSs of Karnataka followed by WDCSs of Andhra Pradesh (46.94), 43.95 for NON-STEP WDCSs of Karnataka, and 37.30 for NON-STEP WDCSs of Andhra Pradesh.

Chapter 8

Women and Self-Help Groups

An attempt is made in this chapter to provide genesis and development of SHGs in India, and to document working of women managed self-help groups in the study area. SHGs are being organised in the area by Government, NGOs, cooperatives, banks, and women themselves. As of Karnataka, women SHGs are organised under Stree Shakti and there are about 50000 such SHGs (ENS, 2001).

Background

Credit is a crucial input in the process of development. For historical reasons, Indian farming community failed to make huge investments in agriculture. There is a saying that 'Indian farmer is born in debt, lives in debt, and dies in debt'. In order to mitigate the problems of farming community, Indian Cooperative Societies Act was passed in 1904. A number of credit cooperatives were started under this Act which provided institutional support to farmers for short, medium and long term purposes. Subsequently, tiers at state and district levels were too conceived to strengthen these credit cooperatives. Apart from these cooperative institutions, nationalisation of commercial banks, and introduction of regional rural banks also helped in increasing credit supply to farmers. As mentioned above, by now the Indian credit cooperatives have a century long history. During this period these institutional financing agencies failed, to a large extent, to meet the requirements (consumption and production) of the farmers. Some of the factors responsible for their failure are inadequate supply of credit, poor recovery, demand-supply gaps, interference by politicians, lack of monitoring, mis-utilization of credit, problems in identification of target group, high transaction costs, lags in time, natural calamities, and above all presence and competition from informal credit agencies. A number of committees (Rural Banking Inquiry Committee (1949), All India Rural Credit Survey Committee (1954), Committee on Cooperative Credit (1960), All Indian Rural Debt and Investment Survey (1962), All India Rural Credit Review Committee (1969), Working Group on Rural Banks (1975), Committee to Review Arrangements for Institutional Credit for Agriculture and Rural Development (1981), Agricultural Credit Review Committee (1989), and Narasimhan (1991 and 1998) constituted by Government of India looked into their working and made several recommendations to improve their health and functioning. Of the total credit provided by these institutions 44% was met by cooperative banks, and 48% by commercial banks leaving a paltry amount by regional rural banks. Till date, these institutions are catering to about 60% of the total credit requirements of farmers.

Government Support

In order to provide refinancing to cooperatives, commercial banks, and regional rural banks, NABARD was created in 1982. These institutions, despite various governmental assistance, failed to meet the requirements of farmers. Further, the above structures did not cater to the landless, marginalized, and disadvantaged groups. With a view to provide some relief to these groups of people, a concept called micro financing was promoted. The genesis of SHGs could be traced to mutual aid in Indian village community. Self-help in essence is a form of cooperation. Cooperatives are formal bodies, whereas SHGs are informal (NABARD 1996). Self-help, and reliance are strategies of survival for poor as well as their development from below (Rao, 1994).

Salient features of micro finance are to provide access to credit to poor (men and women) with no collateral obligations. It encourages savings and promote income generating activities.

Loans are provided at the market driven rates of interest and peer pressure is used in repayment. This micro finance is carried out through self help groups where poor come together in the range of 10-20 through weekly, fortnightly, and monthly meetings through their savings and loaning. It is hoped that through such interventions hitherto uncovered groups are covered with credit and in the process they are empowered. The experiences available in the country and elsewhere suggest that they are (SHGs) sustainable, have replicability, stimulate savings, and in the process helped borrowers to come out of the vicious circle of poverty. Some of the benefits of women's SHGs are: (1) inculcation of spirit of self-effort and self-reliance among women, (2) enabling a forum for women to exchange ideas, and experiences, (3) providing opportunities to women to encourage in productive work, (4) fostering spirit of cooperation among women, (5) promoting awareness, (6) providing opportunities to acquire skills, and (7) providing confidence (Jha, 2001).

International Network

In this context, a mention about the World Micro Credit Summit, 1997 is in order. The Summit held at Washington DC resolved to reach 100 million poorest families by 2005. The Summit concluded that aid programmes often failed to reach poorest 20% of the population. There are about 1.3 billion absolute poor in the world and of this 900 million are women. India and China account for 20% of the world's poorest. There are few successful micro financing models in India and elsewhere and they include Grameen Bank, Association for Social Advancement, Women Entrepreneurship Development, Bangladesh Rural Advancement Committee (Bangladesh), Bank Rakyat (Indonesia), Pag-IBAG-fund (Philippines), etc. These institutions have formed a network at the international level too.

Role of NABARD

As regards micro finance in India, it is a new concept, perhaps influenced by the success of Grameen Bank of

Bangladesh. Apart from Government of India, NABARD, and Rashtriya Mahila Kosh4 have been promoting self-help groups through non-governmental organisations (NGOs) and banks. Self-help group is a small economically homogeneous and affinity group of rural poor voluntarily formed to save and mutually agree to contribute to a common fund to be lend to its members as per groups decision. The great merit of SHGs has been their ability to inculcate among members sound habits of thrift, savings, and banking. Self -help groups or micro credit groups have been recognised as useful tools to help poor access financial resources not available to them previously and help them break through the stronghold of exploitative moneylenders.

There is an in built conflict resolution mechanism in SHGs and cent percent repayment is ensured through peer pressure. According NABARD (1994), there are five stages (pre-formation, formation, stabilization (phase 1), stabilization (phase 2), and growth and expansion) in the development of SHGs (Table 8.1). Time period required and focus of activities in each stage are also provided in the table.

Table 8.1

Stages of SHG Development and Role of NGOs/SHPI*

Stage of development	*Time period*	*Role of NGO/SHPI*	*Focus of activities*
Pre-formation	1-2 months	Initiator/ Promoter	Identifying the poor through participatory rural appraisal methods in small hamlets/ villages/towns.
Formation	3-6 months	Facilitator	Motivation to form groups, select group leaders, develop rules and norms, conduct meetings, pooling savings, issue and collection of small loans, group cohesion, adjustment systems, and maintenance of accounts.

(Contd.)

Stage of development	*Time period*	*Role of NGO/SHPI*	*Focus of activities*
Stabilization (Phase 1)	7-12 months	Advisory/ Managerial	Leadership stabilization, training of leaders and members, regularized and increase savings, handling of groups level transactions, informal interactions with other groups/clusters, addressing community interests. Begin the process of issuing loans, handling/helping defaulters to repay. Sourcing loans for groups through normal credit system, etc.
Stabilization (Phase 2)	13-18 months	Advisory/ Managerial	In addition to above activities, initiation of income generating programmes, linkages of banks', support to new groups, demonstrative effect on others to form groups.
Growth and expansion	19 months and above	Advisory/ Manage-rial/consul-tative/insti-tution build-ing	Strengthen linkages with banks, creation of assets for groups and members, spreading concept building and promotion of new groups, attempts at cluster development, and federation of SHGs.

* SHPI = Self-help promoting institutions.

Source: NABARD (1994).

India Collective for Micro Financing (ICMF) has resolved to cover two million poor women through micro financing by the year 2005. NABARD has planned to link one million SHGs by 2008. Currently about 1 lakh SHGs have been linked through various banks under the aegis of NABARD for which it has refinanced Rs. 150 crores to the banks. Within this overall objective, NABARD and Rashtriya Mahila Kosh have their own specific objectives. There are 3 SHG models tried in India at the moment: (a) bank-SHGs (NGO as a promoter and guarantor), (b) bank-NGOs-SHGs (bank as intermediary), and (c) bank-SHGs (directly by banks).

SHG-Bank Linkage Programme

With a view to facilitate smoother and meaningful banking with the poor, a pilot project for purveying micro credit by linking SHGs with banks was launched by NABARD in 1991-92. Reserve Bank of India (RBI) had then advised commercial banks to actively participate in this linkage program. The scheme has since been extended to RRBs and cooperative banks. As against a target of 50000 SHGs envisaged in the Union Budget, 81780 SHGs received micro credit from banks during 1999-2000. A target of 1.00 lakh SHGs was set for 2000-01 for linkage by banks. The number of SHGs linked to banks aggregated to 1.50 lakhs by the end of 2000-01. This translates into an estimated 1.9 million very poor families brought within the fold of formal banking services. More than 85% of the groups linked with banks are 'exclusive women' groups. While cumulative disbursement of bank loans to these SHGs stood at Rs. 193 crores as on March 31, 2000, refinance of Rs. 150.10 crores have been drawn by banks against 94,645 credit linked SHGs. 40 commercial banks (including 13 from private sector), 165 RRBs, and 61 cooperative banks are now associated with the SHG-bank linkage program.

Status of SHGs in India

Most of the self help-groups of the country are concentrated in southern India and about 29000 are in Andhra Pradesh alone, followed by Tamil Nadu, Karnataka, and Maharashtra. However, as many as 7670 are also working in Uttar Pradesh. About 90% these groups cover 'women only'. There are number of micro financing institutions in India, and prominent among them are NABARD, PRADHAN, WWF, SEWA, CDF, MYRADA, ADITHI, etc. The concept was introduced in India sometime in 1985 and during this period NABARD and several individual researchers carried out impact studies of self-help groups [NABARD (1989), Kumaran (1997), NABARD (1995), AARO (1998), Hussain (1999), Jha (2000), Kumaran (1999),

Puhazhendhi and Jayaraman (1999), Choudhury, et.al. (2000), Jha (2000), Kulshrestha (2000), Raman (2000), Kasar, et al. (2001), Ojha (2001), and Rajagopalan (2001)]. These studies concluded that SHGs helped in improving socio-economic conditions of members. Major factors which helped these SHGs are: (a) socio-economic homogeneity of the group, (b) small size, (c) functionality, (d) participation, (e) voluntary mode, (f) non-political nature, and (g) above all similarities of needs and problems of group members.

Status of SHGs in the Study Area

As discussed earlier, study covered 48 WDCSs spread over six districts of Andhra Pradesh and Karnataka. These 48 villages have 23 SHGs (Table 8.2). Highest percentage of SHGs are noticed from STEP area of Karnataka followed by STEP region of Andhra Pradesh. Non-STEP WDCSs of Andhra Pradesh have lowest percentage of SHGs. Average membership/group hovered around 15 in both the states.

Table 8.2
Coverage of SHGs by WDCSs

State	*Sample WDCSs*	*WDCSs having SHGs*	*% of SHGs organised*	*Average membership*
Andhra Pradesh				
STEP	12	6	50.0	15
NON-STEP	12	4	33.3	17
Total	24	10	41.7	15
Karnataka				
STEP	12	8	66.7	16
NON-STEP	12	5	41.7	14
Total	24	13	54.2	15

Source: Field study.

These SHGs are promoted by government agencies, NGOs, WDCSs, banks, and women themselves (Table 8.3). Out of eight SHGs organised in the STEP area of Karnataka, three are promoted by WDCSs, two by government agencies, and one each by NGO, women, and bank. As of STEP area of Andhra Pradesh, two each are promoted by government, NGOs, and WDCSs. All the selected SHGs are less than two years old (Table 8.4) and majority of them are below one year.

Table 8.3

Agencies Promoted SHGs

Agency	*Andhra Pradesh*		*Karnataka*	
	STEP	*NON-STEP*	*STEP*	*NON-STEP*
1. Government	2	1	2	1
2. NGOs	2	1	1	1
3. WDCSs	2	0	3	2
4. Self	0	1	1	1
5. Banks	0	1	1	0
Total	6	4	8	5

Source: Field study.

Table 8.4

Age of the SHGs

Age	*Andhra Pradesh*		*Karnataka*	
	STEP	*NON-STEP*	*STEP*	*NON-STEP*
less than 6 months	2	1	3	2
6-12 months	2	3	3	2
13-18 months	1	0	1	1
19-24 months	1	0	1	0
	6	4	8	5

Source: Field study.

As mentioned earlier, all 23 SHGs are selected for the study. Initially, women were suspicious in joining the SHGs as they had bitter experiences with such promises earlier. When they were explained about the objectives and mechanics of functioning groups, women came forward and convinced some of their neighbors too. Thirty respondents each are interviewed from STEP and NON-STEP areas of Andhra Pradesh, and Karnataka. All of them were given training in book keeping, leadership, and awareness. Average age of the respondents varied between 32.5 years in STEP areas of Karnataka to 51.0 years in NON-STEP areas of Andhra Pradesh (Table 8.5). Caste-wise distribution of members revealed that more than half of them belonged to SCs/STs, followed by BCs, and FCs. About 35% of them in Andhra Pradesh and 45% in Karnataka are literates. Size of the family varied between 5.3 in STEP areas of Karnataka to 6.2 in NON-STEP areas of Andhra Pradesh. Average/annual income of respondents is the highest in STEP region of Karnataka and the lowest in NON-STEP areas of Andhra Pradesh. Thus, members of STEP areas of Karnataka are young, with lower family sizes, and higher annual incomes. These observations are in concurrence with the earlier findings.

Table 8.5

Profile of Members of SHGs

Particulars	*Andhra Pradesh*		*Karnataka*	
	STEP	*NON-STEP*	*STEP*	*NON-STEP*
1. Age (years)	42.5	51.0	32.5	40.2
2. Caste (%)				
a. SCs/STs	53.4	53.3	53.3	66.6
b. BCs	33.3	40.0	36.7	26.7
c. FCs	13.3	6.7	10.0	6.7
3. Literate (%)	40.0	36.7	46.7	43.3
4. Size of the family	5.8	6.2	5.3	5.9
5. Average income (Rs/annum)	10560	10475	27680	15370

Source: Field study.

Table 8.6

Reasons for Joining SHGs

Reason	*Andhra Pradesh*		*Karnataka*	
	STEP (n=30)	*NON-STEP (n=30)*	*STEP (n=30)*	*NON-STEP (n=30)*
1. Avail credit	7	9	5	7
2. Develop saving habit	6	5	9	8
3. Meet unexpected demand for cash	5	7	7	6
4. Peer pressure	2	4	2	4
5. Motivated by officials/NGOs	2	1	0	0
6. Solidarity	3	2	1	2
7. Exchange of ideas/experiences	2	2	0	1
8. Attend adult education classes	2	0	2	1
9. Empowerment	1	0	4	1

Source: Field study.

When asked about reasons for joining SHG, members cited as many as nine reasons (to avail credit, developing saving habit, to meet unexpected demand for cash, peer pressure, motivated by NGOs/officials, solidarity, exchange of ideas/experiences, attend adult education classes, and empowerment) (Table 8.6). Among all the reasons mentioned, 'to avail credit', 'to meet unexpected demand for cash', and 'develop saving habit' are the prime factors to join the SHGs. However, there are minor variations across various categories of women.

Table 8.7
Working of SHGs

Particulars	*Andhra Pradesh*		*Karnataka*	
	STEP (n=30)	*NON-STEP (n=30)*	*STEP (n=30)*	*NON-STEP (n=30)*
1. Meetings/month	4	2	3	3
2. Savings (Rs./month)	100	75	150	100
3. Total savings (Rs. lakhs)	1.05	0.53	1.90	0.74
4. Rate of interest (%)	24-30	22-36	24-36	24
5. Having linkage with bank	2	1	4	1
6. Repayment (%)	98.5	96.0	100.0	98.5

Source: Field study.

Regular meetings, compulsory attendance, and savings are the features of the SHG. These meetings are conducted at the group leader's house either weekly or fortnightly or thrice a month depending on the convenience of the members (Table 8.7). There is a penalty for late attendance, and absenteeism. Thus, there is 100% participation. Agenda items included savings, flow of credit, income generating activities, recovery, social issues, etc.

Depending on the economic status of the group, women saved Rs. 75 to Rs. 150/month. Total savings of these 23 SHGs is around Rs. 4.22 lakhs and highest amount is saved by STEP members from Karnataka. Generally, after 5-6 months of operation, savings are used for internal lending. The amount of loan and number of loanees are decided by the members depending on the savings, need, and urgency. Loans are sanctioned at 22-36% rate of interest generally for periods ranging between 4-12 months. Women suddenly realised that they have not only access to but control over an amount which they had never dreamt in their lives they would ever see. They opened bank accounts in the name of group to ensure safety of money saved and to access more mainstream credit.

Table 8.8

Purpose-wise Utilization of Loans Taken from SHGs

Purpose	*Andhra Pradesh*		*Karnataka*	
	STEP	*NON-STEP*	*STEP*	*NON-STEP*
1. Consumption credit	10	13	2	5
2. Children's education	3	3	2	0
3. Health	6	2	4	3
4. Social functions	4	1	8	4
5. Purchase of inputs for agriculture	0	2	6	7
6. Petty trade	5	3	6	5
7. Repairs to house	0	2	1	2
8. Repaying old debts	2	4	1	4

Source: Field study.

Purpose-wise utilization of loans taken from SHGs are provided in Table 8.8. 'Credit for consumption' is the major purpose in Andhra Pradesh while it is 'social functions' and 'purchase of inputs for agriculture' in Karnataka. Petty trade is another reason for which loans are borrowed among all the respondents. These groups are also linked with banks to undertake income generating activities through which women could achieve economic independence, and self confidence to some extent.

Thus, women who are belonging to lowest strata of the society are getting habituated to savings and managing SHGs efficiently. Their meetings are conducted regularly with full democratic participation and women are now able to raise small loans from their own savings. Respondents are happy with functioning of SHGs because they inculcated a sense of belongingness, habit of thrift, and discipline among participating members. Further, neither women now need to approach money lenders who provide loans at exorbitant rates of interest nor approach bank who do not fit into their requirements/interests.

Some of these groups are already involved in creating social awareness by composing poems on AIDS, dowry, nutrition, legal literacy, sanitation, multiple roles of women, etc. They got these poems printed and distributed among members and such poems are sung during meetings. Since they are occupied most of the day, visitors particularly researchers/advisors, are requested to visit the groups during nights and started collecting a token amount of Rs. 500-600/meeting as fees for sparing their valuable time. They became time conscious too. Experiences gained in managing WDCSs came handy to these women in organising SHGs efficiently from the very beginning.

Summary

A review of genesis and development of SHGs in India revealed that the existing formal financial institutions failed to provide finances to landless, marginalized, and disadvantaged groups. The origin of SHGs could be traced to mutual aid in Indian village community. Cooperatives are formal bodies, whereas SHGs are informal. SHGs encourages savings and promote income generating activities through small loans. The experiences available in the country and elsewhere suggested that SHGs are sustainable, have replicability, stimulates savings, and in the process helped borrowers to come out of vicious circle of poverty. There are a number of successful micro-financing agencies in India and abroad. These institutions have formed a network at the international level. Apart from Government of India, NABARD, and Rashtriya Mahila Kosh have been promoting self-help groups through NGOs and banks. So far about 2 million very poor families are brought within the fold of formal banking services. Most of the SHGs of the country are concentrated in southern Indian. A number of research studies carried out to find out the impact of SHGs revealed that they helped in improving socio-economic conditions of members.

There are 23 SHGs in the study area and majority of them are located in STEP areas in Karnataka. All the groups members were given training in book keeping, leadership, and awareness. Average age of the respondents varied between 32.5 years in STEP areas of Karnataka to 51 years in NON-STEP areas of Andhra Pradesh. Most of the members are SCs/STs with a literacy of a 45%. As of reasons for joining SHGs, members cited that 'to avail credit', 'to meet unexpected demand for cash', and 'develop saving habit' as prime factors. Women with following backgrounds became involved in SHGs: (a) who are widowed or divorced, (b) whose families have no adult male earning members, (c) whose husbands cannot afford family expenditure, (d) whose household sizes are very big, and whose household economic conditions are very poor, (e) who have a strong willingness to improve their economic conditions, and (f) who are able to get husbands' cooperation. Regular meetings, compulsory attendance, and savings are the features of SHGs. Agenda items included savings, flow of credit, income generating activities, recovery, social issue, etc. Depending upon the economic status of group, women saved Rs. 75 to Rs. 150/month. Loans are sanctioned at 22-36% rate of interest generally for periods ranging between 4-12 months. 'Credit for consumption' is the major purpose for which loans are availed in Andhra Pradesh, while it is 'social functions' and 'purchase of inputs for agriculture' in Karnataka. Some of the groups already involved in creating social awareness by composing poems/stories on AIDS, dowry, nutrition, legal literacy, sanitation, multiple roles of women, etc. Experiences gained in managing WDCSs came handy to these women in organising SHGs efficiently from the very beginning.

Chapter 9

Profiles of Selected Women

With a view to provide more insights into socio-economic backgrounds, and individual empowerment scores, an attempt is made in this chapter to provide profiles of 16 dairy women drawn from both Andhra Pradesh and Karnataka. Selection of these cases is based on impressions of the researcher, cooperation extended by women during interviews, and peculiar nature of respondents. Efforts are taken to cover women from all sections of society from both the states. Some of the names of respondents are changed, wherever necessary, to conceal identity.

Venkata Ramana

Ms. Venkata Ramana aged thirty seven is a self-made chairperson exudes confidence and repose faith in her bright future. She hails from a forward caste community from Prakasam district of Andhra Pradesh. She is one of the seven sisters of her parents who are illiterate. She studied up to 12th standard in a RCM High School in 1982 and got married at the age of 19. Ms. Ramana participated in NCC and a state level basket ball player in her school days. Her husband is a landlord and Ms. Ramana too has three acres of her own. She has two daughters and the eldest is doing medicine while the youngest aspiring for engineering. Her visits to natal village is usually restricted to ritual occasions (marriages, social functions, naming ceremony, etc.). The village had a bad experience of experimenting with a number of milk societies but all of them failed due to political reasons. Taking this as an advantage milk vendors too cheated them. It was in 1994 that Ms. Ramana motivated women folk and with the help of officials of the milk union, a WDCS was organised and registered in a record period of five months. Members belong to other party tried their level best to ruin this WDCS and finally she succeeded in keeping the members together, and running the WDCS in profits. Slowly procurement increased and society provided security to get bank loans for purchasing milch animals. Genuine and sincere women were selected for the loans and all of them repaid promptly. Thus, she is instrumental in organising and managing the WDCS.

Initially there was difficulty in getting sincere and trained women to work as secretary, and tester, but those problems were set right. Ramana attended several training programmes at Anand, Erode, Vijayawada, Chittoor, etc. Other women too were trained to look after various activities of the WDCS. Meetings are conducted regularly in their society. Ramana is also group leader of the SHG, has a savings account and has no regrets in having daughters. In fact she is proud of two daughters who are good at studies as also extra curricular activities. According to Ramana, 'a daughter is better than a son because even after marriage daughter shares the same rapport with the parents. Unlike boys, who tend to overlook their parents after marriage, daughters have more love and affection towards parents'. She does not believe in the 'other world' and decided to have last rites with daughters only. She opined that 'a woman thinks better with both head and heart while man is more inclined towards just the head'. She visits the society regularly and has been successful to in getting a PHC, high school, and bus to the village. She is aware of the reservation policy for women and would like to contest for post of panchayat president in the coming election. Ramana is very much thankful to her husband who is supportive, understanding, and cooperative. She requested for frequent training programmes to other members of the WDCS, and regular and reasonable payment for the milk. In her opinion 'women attend lot of work at home and outside and it is not recognized. Women not only get unequal pay for equal work but many jobs that women attend are categorised as low skilled for which low wages are paid. But this injustice is to end and we are fighting for it'. Her empowerment score is 64.

Renukamma

Ms. Renukamma is a backward caste woman from Chittoor district and aged forty. She studied up to 10th standard and wished to continue but her father decided to get her married. She succeeded in getting a husband who is a small farmer, and studied up to 12th standard. She is living in a supplemented nuclear family and according to her 'marriage is precious and a must for women'. Her natal village is eighty two kilometers away and visited thrice last year for attending village festival, Sankranti, and Vijaya Dasami. She owns two crossbred cows, has a saving account, and member of a SHG. Renukamma has just finished serving lunch to her teenage son and sitting with a neighbour when we walked in. She lends money to neighbours without the knowledge of her husband who is mostly busy with farming. By the time we finished our interview, Renukamma's daughter came back from the nearby town after attending her college. She served us idly, tea, and water. Our discussions went around WDCS, and her role in the house/WDCS. She has been an active member of the WDCS, and member of management committee. She is well versed with society's activities (conduct of meetings, annual general meetings, maintenance of records, fat test, accounting, etc.). Renukamma attended a number of training programmes and visited Anand, Chittoor dairy, Tirumala, and Madras. Her husband is understanding and helpful and she excepts similar 'cooperation and non-interference from village elders' so as to manage WDCS efficiently. According to her, 'WDCS is a business organisation and profits and members participation should be the indicators for measuring success of a WDCS'. As milk payments are pending for the last 45 days, she is not happy with the management of Chittoor union. She expects the management to follow business principles and make employees responsible for their actions. Renukamma is against frequent transfers to CEOs. She is happy with STEP programme and confident of managing WDCS even after discontinuation of facilities. Renukamma felt that 'women are already bearing reproductive burden (having to deliver children and to look after them). In addition, they have to take care of families, agriculture, animal husbandry, etc. Why cannot government popularize male sterilization?' Her empowerment score is 60.

Veerakumari

Ms. Veerakumari is a Kamma community woman from Chittoor district. She was married to a medium sized farmer at the age of seventeen. It was an arranged marriage and her parents gave a dowry of 100 gms. gold, Rs. 2 lakhs in cash, and an acre of wet land. Being an educated woman (10th standard), Kumari found no difficulty in adjusting with her in-laws and husband. Her husband being the only son to her in-laws, she enjoyed maximum liberty in the house. Since there are very few facilities in the village, Kumari advised her husband to shift to a nearby town so that two children can be provided education facilities. Her husband liked the idea and left mother who is widow in the village. Kumari visits the village, and WDCS, once in a week and keep herself abreast about the developments. The actual work related to milch animals is being taken care of by her mother-in-law while she is the member of the WDCS. She also collect money from the WDCS and spend it for various household purposes. She said that the milk union should improve procurement by supplying quality technical inputs on regular basis and paying reasonable price for the milk. Her monthly average income from the sale of milk is Rs. 900 of which is 50% goes towards feed, and other expenses. Once she attended the annual general body meeting of the union and would like to visit Anand. She proposed to make her children bank employees and would like to settle in the town but at the same time keep in touch with village. Her empowerment score is 51.

Bharatamma

Ms. Bharatamma is forty years old and a dairy farmer in her own way and belong to Warangal district. She studied up to 9th standard and a got married at the age of eighteen. Her husband is a small farmer and owner of a provision shop. She has two daughters and a son. Daughter is doing B.E. (Electronics and Telecommunication), son pursuing B.E. (Chemical Engineering), and the youngest is in 9th standard. She cooks mostly vegetarian food but non-vegetarian (fish/meat/chicken) is a must on Sunday. Average annual income of their family is Rs. 85,000. Initially she stayed with in-laws but later developed difference of opinion with them. She persuaded husband to settle in her natal village so that her parents can come to rescue in case of difficulties. Sankara, husband, reluctantly agreed to this proposal. They purchased three acres of wet land with their share of property as also two crossbred cows. Bharatamma took care of lands and animals while Sankara looked after the provision shop. Due to her active involvement and father's influence, she became member of the management committee, Director of the PACS, and also undertaking small contract works in the village. She is now interested in contesting for chairperson of WDCS and very much confident about it. She has not attended any training programme so far and would like to visit Amul. When asked about son is better or daughter, she said that 'it is not fair to give a biased judgement. Girls and boys are equal in terms of tackling problems and shouldering responsibilities. It all depends as how parents nurture and mould them into responsible adults'. They have a saving of Rs. 1.50 lakhs and her priorities are arranging marriage to elder daughter and constructing a pucca house. Ms. Bharatamma gave the following details about economics of two crossbred cows (Table 9.1). Ms. Bharatamma's empowerment score is 46.

Table 9.1

Economics of Crossbred Cows

Particulars	*Amount (Rs./year)*
Milch yield @ 10 months/animal 6 liters x 4 months 4.5 liters x 4 months 3 liters x 2 months	
Total milk production (litres/year)	2880
Sold to WDCS (litres)	2155
Sale value of milk (@ Rs. 8.5/litres)	18317
Cost of concentrates (@ Rs.15/animal/day)	9000
Cost of home grown fodder (greens/dry)	2500
Cost of medicines	350
Net returns	6467

Mehrunnisa

Ms. Mehrunnisa is 46 years old and ardent believer of marriage system. She belong to Warangal district of Andhra Pradesh. Ms. Mehrunnisa got married at the age of 15. All the three elements of Muslim marriage (Nikah) were followed in her case: (a) marriage proposal was made by parents, (b) acceptance of proposal in the presence of few relatives, and (c) settlement of Dower or Mehar (a particular sum of money or property which the bride is entitled to receive from bridegroom in consideration of marriage). Husband has 4 acres of land, 3 improved buffaloes, and petty business. Both the in-laws expired soon after her marriage and since then staying in a nuclear family. They have two daughters and have two sons, both daughters married while sons continuing education. She treat all the four equally without any discrimination. Income from petty business is sufficient for the maintenance of her family and income from dairying (Rs. 20000) is a saving. According the her, 'education has become a money making business and people like us are unable to meet the expenses'.

She is a god fearing woman and according to her Islam means 'submission to the will of Allah'. Her husband respects her views and encouraged to join WDCS and SHG. She is on the management committee and has many Hindus friends. She visits her friends houses, meetings, etc. They all live like a close nit family and she gets lot of respect from Hindu friends too. She is not happy with the current procurement of the WDCS and would like to increase up to 500 litres/day. She proposes to provide bank guarantee to poor women so that they can purchase graded buffaloes. She celebrates both Id-Ul-Fitr and Bakr-Id with devotion and enthusiasm and distributes sweets to Hindus friends. Her empowerment score is 45.

Mariamma

Ms. Mariamma belong to Warangal district, landless, and scheduled caste woman converted into Christianity. She studied up to 4th standard and left the school unwillingly at the age of ten to look after her younger brother. Her step-father did not consider it worthwhile to educate a girl child who can work at home. 'Being in school means forgoing opportunity to earn or help in the home, thereby releasing adults for productive activity. In a poverty situation, the costs in real terms are too high and schooling is seen as a poor investment which provides no sure access to better employment'. Mariamma's husband works as an agricultural labour. She has two local buffaloes and have two sons who work as a helpers on some one else's land. As a part of the agreement, they can look after their own buffaloes alongwith those of the employer. Their annual income is Rs. 28500. Her husband decides on purchase of milch animals, feeds, vaccination, use of artificial insemination for milch animals, receives milk payment, and decides on the use of money earned from milk sales.

Mariamma relishes vegetarian food while husband is fond of non-vegetarian diet. She has no saving account of her own and husband is an alcoholic. He spends 1/4th of the income on liquor. According to her, 'women attend lot of work at home but it is not recognised. We work long and tedious hours, but eat after men and boys in our house. It is assumed that men need better and more nutritious food because they work hard and are the bred winners'. When asked about the preference towards son or daughter, she mentioned that 'although I have caring sons, I can certainly say without doubt that a daughter is better any day because she is more sincere and caring towards her parents. Many a times it happens the moment a son get married, he becomes a hen-pecked husband'. Her empowerment score is 32.

Sarojini

Ms. Sarojini is of fifty years old and belong to a backward caste community. Sarojini who hails from Prakasam district studied up to 4th standard and got married at the age of fifteen. Her natal village is 30 kms. away and she had little contacts with brother/sister. She has three sons and a daughter, all except the younger son got married. She has neither personal savings nor milch animal of her own. Her husband is working as a clerk in the electricity department. She was little known in the village prior to membership in the WDCS. Her participation in WDCS and later on a member of managing committee provided an opportunity to become a Director of the PACS. In the process of upward movement in the social hierarchy, Sarojini who had been attending manual agriculture work, withdrew from such 'outside' work. On an average, they get Rs. 7500 from milk sales and mostly it is given to husband.

When asked about philosophy of life, she mentioned that as opportunity seldom comes knocking on your door, one must grab every opportunity to make the most of it. She is tradition bounded and felt that girls should not have freedom to marry of their choice and in favour of arranged marriages. She likes son compared to daughter as she expect to depend upon him during old age. When neighbours contacted to join SHG, she declined the proposal. Most of the things in her house are decided by husband and she meekly follow his instructions. Her empowerment score is 30.

Jayantamma

Ms. Jayantamma belong to Brahmin community and completed her graduation (B.Com.). Her father worked as a Police Sub Inspector and Jayantamma was born and brought up in Bangalore. She got married to maternal uncle at 22 when she was working with a nationalised bank. Since husband is settled in village, she was forced to resign and join him. Husband is having business and fairly respectable person in the village. With her educational background, Jayantamma started showing interest in politics and social service. In fact her contribution towards upliftment of the poor has been going on since she was 12. She could not bear the pains of poor. She had her own group and approach social service organisations working towards betterment of poor. She participated in blood donation camps, adult education programmes, undertook tree plantation, sanitation, etc.

They have five acres of irrigated land and another 5 acres of unirrigated land. She has two sons both studying in upper primary school and a servant to look after the household chores and animals. Jayantamma saw the problems women in carrying milk to a nearby dairy society. She decided to organise one such society in their village. Being a active member of the congress party, she hardly faced any problem in arranging meetings and organising a WDCS. She attended number of training programmes at Bangalore, Yelhanka, Solur, Vaskote, Anekal, etc. She feels that there is lot of scope for improving procurement of the society. There are number of private dairies operating in the village. According to her fat test is not carried out regularly but she is happy about the facilities extended by the union. She has saving account and Rs. 10000 on her name. She is member of many organisations like: grampanchayat, primary marketing society, taluka level marketing society, district school board, vice-president of rural high school, and general secretary of district level congress party. When asked about status of women in the society, she mentioned that 'we have kept women out of the mainstream of the society and over period they have developed the capacity to internalize injustices. Bias is deep rooted and constitutional provisions are not handy to address discrimination against women. Law is not a panacea but it is only a catalyst. Removal of ignorance through education is the need of the hour and STEP is a wonderful intervention in that direction'. Her empowerment score is 67.

Sailaja

Ms. Sailaja was born in Guntur district of Andhra Pradesh but got married to her maternal uncle who settled in a camp in Bellary district. She studied up to 12th standard and was good at both studies and athletics. She was interested in continuing education but mother forced her to get married as early as possible. Her husband is having 35 acres of irrigated land in Bellary. They have all modern gadgets in the house and interested in purchasing a maruti car. They have a son and daughter, both are studying in private school. When inquired about her role in organising the WDCS, she narrated an incident which took place in 1995. She was travelling by train from Guntur to Bellary and saw a ticket collector harassing a lady travelling with her four years son. The ticket collector was asking for money as fine for travelling without ticket for her son. According to rules, a ticket is purchased for kids above five years and she snatched the identity card of the ticket collector and gave it back only when he apologised to the lady. They have 4 crossbred cows and supplying 30 litres of milk daily to the WDCS. She expects regular visits by the veterinary doctor and good quality cattle feed at reasonable price. Ms. Sailaja attended number of training programmes and would like to start a self-help group in the camp. She work for about 12 hours a day and is first to get up in the house as also the last to go to bed. Though she admits that there is discrimination against women she is not bothered about it because her husband is cooperative and respects her ideas. 'I am a mother of a son and a daughter from being a wife. Handling two responsibilities (WDCS and family) is not easy but my husband and children have always supported me. Working for the

WDCS is like working for my mother. If I do not respect my mother by being honest in my work how can I expect my children to respect their mother'. Sailaja is in favour of revamping education curriculum. She expressed her concern about illiteracy, poverty, and corruption. Her empowerment score is 61.

Sarojamma

Ms. Sarojamma is forty years old and married to Muniswamy Reddy at the age of sixteen and hails from Belgaum district. They have ten acres of land of which eight acres is under Eucalyptus plantation. Sarojamma has three crossbreds cows, two local cows, and two calves. She pours ten litres of milk daily to society and retains three litres for home consumption. She has three sons of which elder one is married and staying separately in the nearby city. Annual general body meeting and managing committee meetings are conducted regularly in their WDCS. She actively participates in the discussions. She attended number of training programmes at Bangalore, Dharwad, and visited Anand too. According to her 'the trip to Anand did a world of good for me. I learned to communicate with people and my sense of responsibility got better. It is pleasing and interesting to know that a young woman teaching, hygiene, birth control, human nutrition, etc. to her mother's generation'. Accordingly to her 'a forte of women is training'. For women, planning and management of WDCS is a grand opportunity to show their skills at decision making as chairpersons and members of management committee. But they need to be helped with training, exposure, and facilities to promote assertiveness, self-confidence, and confidence in governance. Inclusion of women at policy formulation and implementation levels in this regard would be vital. She expressed her satisfaction about the impact of society on her life. She has a saving bank account and participates in decision making process. Though she has no daughters, she is in favour of sons as one can fall back during old age. Her empowerment score is 57.

Grace Radhamma

Ms. Grace Radhamma is tall, fair, and proud owner of three crossbreds who hails from Bellary district. She is forty five years old and has five acres of irrigated land. She was married to her maternal uncle at the age of sixteen. She has three daughters and a son and all of them are studying in a government high school. Though she was not interested in going to school during childhood, she was forced to because her maternal uncle expressed his desire to marry an educated girl. The youngest of four sisters, Radhamma was a fiery orator during her high school days. She visits the church every Sunday and a god fearing woman. Even though she studied in an all girls school, she felt that co-education is definitely better because 'we live in a society where we can not separate boys from girls and it has its advantages'. According to her, 'mother's work is far heavier than that of father's. This lopsided burden must be corrected and they must stand as equal partners in every activity including decision making. Radhamma enjoys watching serials like Aurat, Banegi Apni Baat, Goomrah, Kahani Ghar Ghar Kii, Khandan, Kusum, Kyun Ki Saas Bhi Kabhi Bahu Thi, Shagun, Shanti, Swabhiman, and Udan. The lead characters in these serials have come out on other own right, breaking all socials barriers, and setting themselves as role models. Her empowerment score is 54.

Vijayalakshmi

Ms. Vijayalakshmi hails from Gudadur village of Bellary district. Vijayalakshmi is born in upper class Reddy family and married to a landlord immediately after she passed 10th standard. She has two daughters and a son and had undergone tubectomy. Majority of the lands in the village are irrigated and Vijayalakshmi owns 3 acres of land which was given by her parents at the time of marriage. Parents also gave two crossbreds and currently she is supplying nine litres of milk daily to the society while three litres are consumed at home. When asked about her marriage she started crying and said that 'I wanted to study further and my father supported me too but my Pedananna (father's elder brother) who presided over our joint family put his feet down'. She is determined that it would not happen in her house. Her daughter is studying B.Sc. (Computers) at the nearby town and firmly told that we will not get her married till she agrees. She is member on the management committee of the WDCS and her aim is that every girl child in the village should go to school and every woman should become member of the SHG, with their own savings bank accounts and income. She has earmarked one acre of wet land for cultivation of green fodder. She attends almost all the works associated with milk production and receives payment from the WDCS. She decides as to purchase/sale of milch animals, artificial insemination, feeds, household matters, etc. Her empowerment score is 54.

Koteswaramma

Ms. Koteswaramma belongs to Ammanakeri village of Bellary district. She is forty five years old and belong to forward caste community. Her husband is a farmer and has 4.50 acres of irrigated land. They have a son and four daughters. While all the daughters are married, the son is doing B.E. Her husband insisted for a son and thus she had five deliveries. Son is 'Vamshodharak' for her. They have a crossbred and a local cow. When asked about her marriage she mentioned that 'when we got married forget seeing each other, we were not even asked whether we were ready for marriage or not. His father and mine got together and decided our marriage. I was 12 and he 23 at that time. Adjustment and mutual understanding are the keys to happiness in a marriage. Those days we could not even talk to each other in front of elders even after years of marriage. If I wanted to take baby from him, he would keep the child down and then I would lift the baby and vice-versa'. Her advise to younger generation is that 'everything happens with time. One must be patient and wait for the right things to happen at the right time. Good things come long soon enough. Be selective and choose judiciously'. Her empowerment score is 52.

Ammayamma

Ms. Ammayamma is fifty years old and belong to a Bhajantri (Backward Caste) community. She hails from Railway Gollahally village of Bangalore rural district. She has seven daughters and a son. Of the eight children, seven are married and the younger daughter is doing 11th. Ammayamma is the second wife to her husband. As her husband had no children from his first wife, who happens to be her elder sister, she was forced to marry her husband. Her sister (co-wife) is 10 years elder to her. She had no qualms in staying with sister and a big family. She is illiterate and opines that her mother was responsible for that situation. Daughters got married to rich people and they in turn helped younger once to get married to better off persons. Ammayamma's son is working in a private hospital and staying separately and never looked after parents. Ammayamma blames her daughter-in-law for all this misfortune. But she is happy because 'son is not asking for money'. On an average, she gave Rs. 1.00 to 1.50 lakhs/ daughter and most of it was contributed by daughters only. She has a crossbred cow and her husband has a saloon shop. Currently, they have an acre of irrigated land. She is very regular in attending general body meetings as also committee meetings. She is aware of the societies objectives, attended number of training programmes but would like to visit Anand dairy. She feels that WDCS has helped in improving her economic and social status. She has a saving of Rs. 2.00 lakhs for arranging youngest daughter's marriage and looking for a good proposal. She expressed her willingness to purchase a crossbred provided a bank loan is given. Ms. Ammayamma has good reputation in the village and runs a small tea shop too. According to her, 'to view men as the enemy is not going to be easy for most women: since it amounts to rejecting the most significant men in their lives like fathers, brothers, and husbands'. She is habituated to listening Bhajans, Kirtans, and watching mythological serials. Work is one thing that she can not do without. She keeps herself busy, enjoy meeting people and talking to them. Her empowerment score is 49.

Jayamma

Ms. Jayamma is forty five years old and stands 5 feet 7 inches in height and belong to Bellary district. She loves her three sons and friends, but like to be independent. She studied up to 12th standard in an English medium school and got married in her natal village to a landlord who is her cross cousin. She is the eldest of the three sisters to her parents. She has two crossbred cows, three murrah buffaloes, and four female calves. All the animals are pregnant at the time of interview. Her gross receipts from the WDCS is around Rs. 28000/year of which 40% is spent on concentrates. Jayamma is aware of the objectives of the society and an active member of management committee. She attended all the 12 committee meetings conducted during the previous year. She is aware of STEP programme and attended number of training programmes at Bangalore, Anand, and Erode. She is confident of managing WDCS and interested in contesting for ensuing Panchayat elections. Ms. Jayamma is satisfied with the services (technical guidance, AI, healthcare, price, etc.) being offered by the WDCS. She felt that her status has improved due to membership in the society. She opined that sensitization and creating awareness about women issues, and giving training to men and women on understanding covert and overt discrimination that exists in the society today would go a long way in improving the harmony. 'Women are better equipped today. They know what they want and they are there is in every field. Education is the main tool to make yourself capable. In this world, education offers an identity and respect. It forms an essence of what you are and who you are. Its quite impossible to think of life without education'. Her empowerment score is 49.

Chandramma

Ms. Chandramma hails from Vokkaliga community and aged forty. She belongs to Belgaum district. She studied up to 8th standard and married to Changappa who is working with electricity department. She has two sons and advised by husband to undergo family planning operation. Initially, the village had no milk society. Ms. Chandramma's husband took interest in organising a WDCS, village elders too supported the idea. They all unanimously elected Chandramma as the chairperson. When asked about her qualities as a chairperson, she told that 'I won the first election simply because my husband is influential in the village but won the second election because I proved to be a good chairperson'. She proposes to have an association of women chairpersons, so that common issues of women chairpersons including oppressions and suppressions by their husbands, village elders, and even district officials can be taken up. 'Since we take a united stand on these issues we invariably prevail'. Tackling husbands is a ticklish problem and should be dealt with respectfully but firmly because we do not want to break families. According to her 'illiteracy and economic dependence are the two major inhibiting factors for non participation of women in developmental activities'. Their annual family income is Rs. 1.75 lakh of which Rs. 25000 is contributed by dairying. In her opinion, 'women have always had the habit of savings for a rainy day. They experience a daily dilemma of consuming versus saving, more than men, as women have to keep the home fires burning'. They have a T.V., refrigerator, scooter, cycle, and other consumable items at their house. Her empowerment score is 47.

Summary

An analysis of case studies of selected women respondents revealed that they are from patrilineal and patri-virilocal systems. Irrespective of religion, marriage is a sacrament for them. It is regarded as a socio-religious duty. Marriages between cross-cousins (centripetal tendency) are allowed and being practised. Educated women not only desired to postpone their marriages to a much a later age but also wanted to marry men with some educational background. Most of them are living in supplemented nuclear families where women have reasonable level of participation in decision making process and bargaining power. They visited natal villages twice/thrice a year for attending certain social ceremonies. Women not only provided care economy but also took responsibility of controlling size of the family by undergoing tubectomy. Majority of them had two children and aspiring to provide equal education to sons and daughters. Some have money in their saving accounts while some have animals and a few of them have land too on their name. Women from high caste Hindu families with relatively large holdings and schooling exerted influence both at home and in WDCS. They are frequently visiting nearby towns and cities/milk union/centres of learning alongwith other members of WDCSs. They have high ambition and willing to put in extra efforts to reach their goals. They are not only concerned about their families but also about the community around them. In majority of the cases, WDCSs helped in providing gainful employment and income. They wanted closer understanding and cooperation from their husbands and requested for non-interference by elders in matters related to WDCSs. They expressed desire to have more training programmes, and awareness camps on a variety of issues pertaining to women. WDCSs opened many avenues as also helped in creating awareness and realizing their inherent power in managing democratic peoples organisations. Women discovered a power in themselves and not feeling dejected.

Chapter 10

Summary and Recommendations

Backdrop

Agriculture is the backbone of Indian economy. Animal husbandry contributes to as much as 25 per cent of the total value of agricultural production. Milk and milk products are the major components in animal husbandry. Encouraged by the success achieved at The Kaira district milk producers' cooperative union limited (Anand), Government of India advocated 'Anand pattern' dairy cooperatives under the aegis of National Dairy Development Board. Organisation of milk cooperatives got fillip during operation flood period (1970-86) and today India is the largest milk producing country in the world. Vast majority of these cooperatives are mixed gender societies. Realising the contribution of women in dairying, the first 'all women dairy cooperatives society' (WDCS) was organised at Khadgodhra (Kaira district) in 1968. Later, other milk unions/federations too started such 'women only' societies. Further, several international agencies (Ford Foundation, Indo-Swiss project, The Netherlands project, etc.) financed organising such WDCSs. Offlate, Department of Women and Child Development of the Ministry of Human Resource Development, Government of India started funding WDCSs under STEP programme. The strength of the programme is in arranging a wide range of training programmes to personnel involved in the implementation and milk producers (women members, committee members, and employees) and in fact 20% of the funds of the projects are earmarked for this purpose. As a result, women are being actively participating in the WDCSs, and enhanced awareness is created. STEP is being implemented in over 10 states in collaboration with respective state level dairy federations. Initial response and results appears to be encouraging.

Objectives

10.2 The overall objective of this study is to understand the nature and impact of STEP programme on women and to draw lessons for future policy exercises. The specific objectives of the study are:

(1) to study performance of 'all women dairy cooperative societies' (WDCSs) in different agro-climatic regions;

(2) to calculate quantitative and qualitative changes in women covered under STEP programme;

(3) to observe the differential decision making pattern of farm women in various animal husbandry tasks;

(4) to develop an empowerment scale for women dairy farmers; and

(5) to document working of self-help groups among respondents.

Methodology

The study is conducted in 3 milk unions each of Andhra Pradesh and Karnataka. Primary data are collected from 240 women members spread over 48 WDCSs of 6 milk unions (Prakasam, Warangal, and Chittoor from Andhra Pradesh, and Bangalore, Belgaum, and Bellary-Raichur from Karnataka). Both primary and secondary data are collected during April 2000—March 2001. The following is the chapter-wise summary of the study.

Profiles of APDDCF and Selected Unions

Andhra Pradesh is one of the largest states of southern India. Organised dairying was taken up in the early 1960s and initially the responsibility rested with a number of organisations.

APDDCF was formed in 1981. It has nine milk unions (Visakha, Godavari, Krishna, Guntur, Prakasam, Nellore, Chittoor, Kurnool, and Nalgonda and Ranga Reddy) and dairies at Anantapur, Mahboobnagar, Medak, Nizamabad, Warangal, and Karimnagar are under its direct control. Indo-Swiss project, Ford Foundation project, The Netherlands project, and NDDB's CD program were implemented in the state for involving women into mainstream dairying. STEP programme is also being implemented since 1997-98. Of the three selected milk unions for the study, Prakasam represents coastal Andhra, Chittoor falls in Rayalaseema, while Warangal is drawn from Telangana region.

Prakasam is one of the backward districts of Andhra Pradesh. Majority of the milk producers in the district are landless agricultural labourers, marginal, and small farmers. The milk union was organised in 1986 with an installed capacity of 80000 litres/day which was further expanded to 3.50 lakh litres/day. The union has 426 DCSs, and 355 milk producers association centres covering 1.06 milk producer members. Capacity utilization of the union is the lowest in the state. Half of the DCSs and the management of the union were superseded in 1999. A number of a private dairies had come up in the district, and union is unable to compete with them. Milk payments were due and, members are unhappy with the union. Women dairy project was taken up in the Markapur division of the district. There are 45 WDCSs with a membership of 1691.

Chittoor is known for its small holdings and crossbred population. Ford Foundation aided women development project was implemented during 1983-87. About 110 WDCSs were organised under this project, but currently most of them are either closed or dysfunctional. The union had its golden period during early 1990s and its average procurement/day was about 2.05 lakh litres during 1991. There has been a steep fall over years and currently hovering around 71000 litres/day (1999-00). Milk payments were pending for 2-3 months, when the researcher visited the union in July 2000. Emergence of private dairies, casual nature of elected management, inappropriate marketing strategies, and non-cooperation from employees made producer members to turn towards private dairies.

Warangal district falls outside the operation flood area and thus was developed under Integrated Dairy Development Project of NCDC. There are about 230 DCSs in the milk shed with a total membership of 18703. It has four MCCs with an installed capacity of 61000 litres/day (1999-00). As the local sales were very low, about 75% of its procurement goes to Hyderabad main dairy and it is posting profits for the last 9 years. WDCSs under STEP programme were taken up in Jangaon area of the milkshed.

Profiles of KMF and Selected Unions

Karnataka has a written history of more than 2000 years. It was formed in 1956 and renamed as Karnataka in 1973. Rice is the main food crop followed by maize, millets, and pulses. Scientific animal breeding was followed for the last 300 years in the state. Dairying in the state is one of the major activities which contributes substantially to the rural economy. Formal efforts for dairy development were started in 1974. Later KDDC was setup and finally KMF was organised in 1984. There are 13 milk unions covering 27 districts and as many as 8299 DCSs with 3.28 lakh pourer membership. Average procurement of milk touched a peak of 17.79 lakh litres/day as against a fluid milk sale of 14.42 lakh litres/day. A number of milk products too are being manufactured and sold under the brand name of Nandini. The federation's turnover is about Rs. 870 crores/ annum. With a view to involve women in dairy activities and to empower women of weak sections, STEP programme is being implemented in all 13 milk unions with the help of Ministry of Human Resources Development, Government of India. The programme is in its second phase (2001-03) now and the results so far have been impressive.

Raichur-Bellary milk union was registered in 1989. The area of operation of the milk union consists of 16 talukas from Bellary, Koppal, and Raichur districts. It has 386 functional DCSs with

42000 membership. Women constituted 28% of the total membership and there are 44 WDCSs in the milkshed. Milk procurement of the union increased from 109.34 lakh litres/annum in 1990-91 to 139.59 lakh litres/annum in 1999-00 and turnover stood at Rs. 17.17 crores.

Belgaum district cooperative milk union was registered in 1985. There are 504 DCSs with 56827 members, and 69 WDCSs with 6099 members. Procurement of the union increased from 58.31 lakh litres/annum in 1985-86 to 205.79 lakh litres/annum in 1999-00, that of sale of fluid milk from 32.81 lakh litres to 167.30 lakh litres during the same period. Half of its milk is sold in Goa. Apart from manufacturing several grades of milk, products like cream, ghee, and peda are prepared here. Turnover of the union is Rs. 29.05 crores in 1999-00. The union has been supplying a number of technical inputs to producer members. There is stiff competition from a number of private dairies and the union's health is not satisfactory.

BAMUL has history of almost 40 years. Over a period of time it is evolved as one of the biggest and best milk unions of southern India. The area of the union comprises of Bangalore urban district (3 talukas) and Bangalore rural district (8 talukas) with a total of 2394 revenue villages. Currently it has 1225 DCSs of which 55 are WDCSs and 72 milk procurement routes with 1.82 lakh members. Its current installed capacity is 10 lakh litres/day. Average procurement/DCS is 431 litres/day and the union is paying Rs. 8.82/litre of cow milk. Average procurement is 4.97 lakh litres/day (1999-00) and 87% of it is sold as fluid milk. The union has been providing a number of production enhancement inputs to milk producers. They include veterinary health care facilities, cattlefeed, artificial inseminations, fodder seeds, guidance, etc. The union got best productivity award in 1998-99 by National Productivity Council for its excellent performance.

Performance of STEP and NON-STEP WDCSs

An analysis of both qualitative and quantitative data on the performance of WDCSs revealed that WDCSs of Karnataka are superior to their counterparts in both states. It is mainly due to their homogeneous character, higher levels of awareness among producer members, management committee members, and employees. This was further strengthened by better financial position and support from the unions in terms of training and supervision. Members of these WDCSs were highly satisfied by the services offered to them. Among all categories of WDCSs studied, NON-STOP WDCSs of Andhra Pradesh failed to live up to members expectation. Majority of the chairpersons of WDCSs are landlords drawn from high caste Hindus and election of chairperson, in most of the cases, is unanimous and ritualistic. Irrespective of the state, employment opportunities in these societies were cornered by well to do members having political affiliations leaving little scope for SCs/STs.

Case Studies of Selected WDCSs

Close observation of four cases studies of WDCSs reveal interesting results. In two out of four WDCSs, an official who hailed from the village informed women about WDCS and helped in getting necessary financial support. Though initially men folk were reluctant, they agreed to organise a WDCS as funds are available under STEP, and their previous experiments failed. Thus, women organised WDCSs with the help of union's officials and men folk. Having entered the business organisations they managed it on sound financial management principles. Young and educated women from high caste Hindus managed to occupy the positions on management committees. As observed in chapter 4, STEP societies are better managed compared to NON-STEP societies. Further, performance of WDCSs of Karnataka is much better than WDCSs of Andhra Pradesh. The WDCS of Karnataka supplied a number of production enhancement inputs than the WDCSs of Andhra Pradesh. In general, women faced number of problems from emerging private dairies and sleeping membership. Further, these problems were compounded by presence of political parties and caste groups.

An Overview of Selected Respondents

An overview of respondents revealed that, on the whole, a quarter of women members belong to landless category in the both states, third of them are marginal farmers and about 50-55% of them maintained one animal. Caste-wise, FCs and SCs/STs each constituted 30% followed by BCs in the study area. Majority of respondents are literate. As regards involvement of members in society's activities, higher percentages of involvement is reported from STEP WDCSs of Karnataka than their counterparts of the study. Data on allocation of time by the respondents indicated that women from Karnataka had put in as much as 13.1 hours/day as against 10.7 hours/day in Andhra Pradesh. Women of STEP WDCSs are spending more time on animal husbandry, while NON-STEP WDCSs spend more time on agriculture. There are large variations in incomes realized among STEP and NON-STEP WDCSs.

Women with age between 21-35, having more than eleven years of schooling, belonging to upper castes, with larger land holdings, and with urban maternal place have high level of participation in decision making. Major sources of awareness about social organisations are self, husband, and neighbours. Government officials have not played their role effectively in creating awareness about organisations among respondents. Those who appreciated the usefulness of the organisations account for a large chunk than those who expressed their ignorance. WDCSs have contributed substantially for the improvement in intake of food, health condition, better clothing, enhanced savings, participation in decision making, and creating awareness.

Empowerment Scales

According to respondents, empowerment means awareness, education, being independent, self-reliance, self-confidence, to stand on own legs, and having cash/property. Of the seven indicators mentioned above, as many as 1/4th of respondents, from both Andhra Pradesh and Karnataka, mentioned that 'awareness' as empowerment. Similarly 1/3rd of the respondents of STEP WDCSs indicated that they are 'fully'/'to some extent' empowered while only 12% of respondents of NON-STEP WDCSs from Andhra Pradesh belong to that category. In all 24 empowerment variables are identified and depending upon the nature, variables are given scores as 1, 2, and 3 or 1 or 3. Thus, the total empowerment score ranged between 24 and 72. Average mean scores, for all the variables considered, are higher for respondents of STEP WDCSs and spread of observations from the mean is less. Average score is the highest (53.62) for STEP WDCSs of Karnataka followed by WDCSs of Andhra Pradesh (46.94), 43.95 for NON-STEP WDCSs of Karnataka, and 37.30 for NON-STEP WDCSs of Andhra Pradesh.

Women and Self-help Groups

A review of genesis and development of SHGs in India revealed that the existing formal financial institutions failed to provide finances to landless, marginalized, and disadvantaged groups. The origin of SHGs could be traced to mutual aid in Indian village community. Cooperatives are formal bodies, whereas SHGs are informal. SHGs encourages savings and promote income generating activities through small loans. The experiences available in the country and elsewhere suggested that SHGs are sustainable, have replicability, stimulates savings, and in the process helped borrowers to come out of vicious circle of poverty. There are a number of successful micro-financing agencies in India and abroad. These institutions have formed a network at the international level. Apart from Government of India, NABARD, and Rashtriya Mahila Kosh have been promoting self-help groups through NGOs and banks. So far about 2 million very poor families are brought within the fold of formal banking services. Most of the SHGs of the country are concentrated in southern India. A number of research studies carried out to find out the impact of SHGs revealed that they helped in improving socio-economic conditions of members.

There are 23 SHGs in the study area and majority of them are located in STEP areas in Karnataka. All the group members were given training in book keeping, leadership, and awareness. Average age of the respondents varied between 32.5 years in STEP areas of Karnataka to 51 NON-STEP areas of Andhra Pradesh. Most of the members are SCs/STs with a literacy of a 45%. As of reasons for joining SHGs, members cited that 'to avail credit', 'to meet unexpected demand for cash', and 'develop saving habit' as prime factors. Regular meetings, compulsory attendance, and savings are the features of SHGs. Agenda items included savings, flow of credit, income generating activities, recovery, social issues, etc. Depending upon the economic status of group, women saved Rs. 75 to Rs. 150/month. Loans are sanctioned at 22-36% rate of interest generally for periods ranging between 4-12 months. Credit for consumption is the major purpose for which loans are availed in Andhra Pradesh, while it is social functions and purchase of inputs for agriculture in Karnataka. Some of the groups already involved in creating social awareness by composing poems/ stories on AIDS, dowry, nutrition, legal literacy, sanitation, multiple roles of women, etc. Experiences gained in managing WDCSs came handy to these women in organising SHGs efficiently from the very beginning.

Profiles of Selected Women

An analysis of case studies of selected women respondents revealed that they are from patrilineal and patri-virilocal systems. Irrespective of religion, marriage is a sacrament for them. It is regarded as a socio-religious duty. Marriages between cross-cousins (centripetal tendency) are allowed and being practised. Educated women not only desired to postpone their marriages to a much later age but also wanted to marry men with some educational background. Most of them are living in supplemented nuclear families where women have reasonable level of participation in decision making process and bargaining power. They visited natal villages twice/thrice a year for attending certain social ceremonies. Women not only provided care economy but also took responsibility of controlling size of the family by undergoing tubectomy. Majority of them had two children and aspiring to provide equal education to sons and daughters. Some have money in their saving accounts while some have animals and a few of them have land too on their name. Women from high caste Hindu families with relatively large holdings and schooling exerted influence both at home and in WDCS. They are frequently visiting nearby towns and cities/milk unions/centres of learning alongwith other members of WDCSs. They have high ambition and willing to put in extra efforts to reach their goals. They are not only concerned about their families but also about the community around them. In majority of the cases, WDCSs helped in providing gainful employment and income. They wanted closer understanding and cooperation from their husbands and requested for non-interference by elders in matters related to WDCSs. They expressed desire to have more training programmes, and awareness camps on a variety of issues pertaining to women. WDCSs opened many avenues as also helped in creating awareness and realizing their inherent power in managing democratic peoples organisations. Women discovered a power in themselves and not feeling dejected.

Recommendations

Recommendations are suggested under three broad headings: STEP program, SHGs, and general, and the following paragraphs are arranged in that sequence. Women are the target group of STEP program, and thus thrust has been given for imparting training in various activities to them. Duration, course curriculum, and training venues are decided as per the need and type of training programme to be conducted. Different training programmes are conducted with the help of trained instructors/extension workers, NGOs, and specialists from various fields. Suggestions are made for strengthening these training programmes provided under STEP and are presented in Table 10.1.

Study material and literature supplied to participants should be more pictorial in nature rather than alphabets. Clay models (at training centre level), and charts with pictures should be prepared to show at education programmes conducted at field level. Regular news bulletins stating the success stories and other information on STEP programme should be published periodically. Quality of training programmes should be ensured rather than the quantity. The above suggestions are made keeping in view of the slogan that "if you educate a man, you educate an individual, but if you educate a woman you educate the entire family".

Table 10.1

Suggested Changes in the Training Curriculum

		At the level of training centre		
Sl. No.	*Name of the programme*	*Existing duration*	*Suggestions*	*Contents*
1.	Managing Committee Training programme	3 days	Duration may be kept as such and should be repeated for newcomers as and when committee changes	Knowledge on business, bylaws, rights, duties and responsibilities of management committee members Preparation of budget/analysis of accounts Meeting procedures such as quorum, agenda, notice, and resolution writing Use of technical inputs for increasing milk production Election procedure/audit ratification
2.	Secretary training on society management	30 days	3 weeks at training centre and one week at the level of WDCS. Stipend may be provided to secretary equivalent to her salary in case the salary is not paid for the training period	Collection procedure, testing, record maintenance/registers, preparation of monthly reports, writing of notice, agenda and proceedings (meeting procedure) Duties, responsibilities, general behavior business, knowledge of technical inputs, election procedure and audit/inspection

(Contd.)

Sl. No.	Name of the programme	Existing duration	At the level of training centre Suggestions	Contents
3.	AI worker trainir.g	Varies from project to project	5 weeks 10 days for AI refresher course	Knowledge on breeds, reproductive organs, symptoms of heat, handling semen, LN2, practical training on AI Related records/reporting Liasioning with department of animal husbandry
4.	First aid training	-do-	2 weeks are sufficient. Incorporation of training on vaccine to poultry, goats, and ducks.	Breeds, common diseases, vaccinations/inoculation, treatment of common cases, record keeping/reporting and knowledge on AI
5.	Dairy animal management training	4 days	These two programmes may be clubbed together and the total duration should be kept as 4 days	Involvement of women in dairy animal management, daily routine work, symptoms of good animals, rearing of calves, symptoms of heat, common disease and their prevention through vaccination, care of pregnant animals.
6.	Training on AH and fodder development	3 days		Cattle insurance/ calf insurance, pricing, testing / functions of society. Balanced cattle feed/ration, benefits of fodders (varieties, cultivation, agronomic practices) Urea straw treatment/hay silage, importance of chaff cutter, its use, etc.
7.	Farmer induction programme	4 days	FIP need not be at Anand but can be organised at nearby project where step programme is successful.	Exposure, interactions, visits to successful projects

At the village level			
1. Women education programme	2 days	Continuous 3 days programme in the village (one day for women education, one day for H.A. programme and another day for L.L. programme) This combined programme may be repeated every year as follow-up programmes as it was for the 1st year	Objectives of WDCS, need for women involvement , 3 tier structure, Anand pattern, benefits of STEP project and functioning of cooperative society. Duties and responsibilities of members, eligibility, etc.
2. Health awareness programme	2 days		Knowledge about SHGs Nutritive foods for all , care of pregnant women, first aid for common diseases Child care/vaccination schedule, cleanliness/ hygiene Family planning and awareness about Aids
3. Legal literacy programme	2 days		Existing legal provisions relating to marriage, divorce, dowry, land holding, harassment, etc. Knowledge on FIR and police station Knowledge of post office, panchayat, courts. block, taluka, district, etc.
4. Male orientation programme	1 days	In some of the states this programme is not being done. As it is highly necessary to sensitize the male members before organising a WDCS, this programme should be done at every state project.	Need for women's involvement and their role in DCS, status of Indian women, and STEP programme to assist women

(Contd.)

At the village level			
5. Women MC members seminar	3 days	The programme should be conducted at a central village combining the MC members of 5 WDCSs for one day.	Knowledge on testing, and pricing: practical on management committee meetings Demonstration of urea straw treatment
6. Chairpersons orientation programme	3 days	No alteration in duration of the programme is proposed	Knowledge on bye-laws Duties and responsibilities Election procedure Accounts/Audit/ procedures for meetings Qualities of ideal president Ideal women dairy cooperatives
7. Medium level functionaries training/ workshop	1 day	Include the officers of other related agencies such as Block, banks, Veterinary Department, NABARD, NGO (associated) etc. Workshop should be at union training centre	
8. Trainers training programme	7 days	Should be conducted by the agency who has expertise on this programme	
9. Health worker (midwife) creche management training	3 days	Should be conducted depending upon the area where it is needed	

The ministry has been providing 90% funds for the implementation of the program. The ministry also circulated funds allocation pattern under STEP programme. However, there is a need to reallocate funding pattern, the suggested pattern is provided in Table 10.2.

Table 10.2

Approved Funding Pattern of STEP Programme (percentages)

Sl. No.	*Purpose*	*Approved*	*Suggested*
I	Administration and project cost	6%	11%
II	Training technical skill and orientation of beneficiaries and project functionaries	20%	25%
III	Infrastructure including marketing support, quality control, and managerial support	25%	20%
IV	Raw material for training (equipment and other material)	25%	20%
V	Establishment and development cooperatives, where required, mobilization and strengthening of field level setup where such support is not available	10%	10%
VI	Support services (wherever such support is not available or not be converged).	8%	8%
VII	Overriding cost	6%	6%
	Total	100%	100%

The following suggestions are made for ministry, state governments, and milk unions.

For the Kind Attention of Ministry

1. There must be provision for mid course correction for reallocation of funds and/or additional funds.
2. The project period should be extended to 4 to 5 years instead of 3 to 4 years (with repetition of training programmes).
3. Accrued interest generated out of funds released by the Ministry may be allowed to be utilized without deduction from total fund allocations.

4. Fund release procedure should be simplified and as far as possible delays may be avoided.
5. Letters from federations/milk unions should be acknowledged promptly by Ministry.
6. All the federations and milk unions be covered under STEP programme. Meetings should be called twice a year (by Ministry) so that federations and milk unions can represent grievances and a grievance redressal mechanism can be worked out.
7. RMK's loan repayment period should be kept at 3 years from the date of loan disbursement.
8. Considering earlier investments and inflation, per capita expenditure on each beneficiary under STEP should be revised to Rs. 7500/annum.
9. Ministry (Government of India) should organize inter-state workshops and exposure programmes to senior officers of the federations and unions so that each state representative can interact and learn from each others experiences.
10. A state level meeting of chairpersons of WDCSs should be arranged so that chairpersons of WDCSs can learn from each others experiences.
11. An inter-state workshop for STEP functionaries (lady extension officers) must be arranged by the ministry so as to share experiences, problems being faced, and to work out a plan of action.
12. Ministry should ensure conducting concurrent evaluation of the projects within 2 years from the sanctioning of the project.
13. Ministry shall call explanation if a particular milk union failed to appoint women as project officials.

For the Kind Attention of State Governments

1. State women development corporations, ST/SC/BC corporations, and DRDAs should support the STEP

by extending financial assistance for creation of infrastructure.

2. State women development corporations should support self-help groups and development of entrepreneurship as well as training without any financial help from federations/unions.
3. State women development corporations should be advised to utilize services and infrastructure created by milk federations/unions under STEP programme.
4. Some of the NGOs without prior experience in the field and with little emphasis on forward and backward linkages, are trying to get the STEP project from the ministry. Hence, it is suggested that ministry should insist on getting a recommendation from the state federations and milk unions in order to avoid duplication of work and misuse of funds in the area.

For the Kind Attention of Federations/Unions

1. Assetless rural women (focus should be given to widows and divorcee and destitute women) to improve their social and economic status.
2. Frequent transfers to officers and staff involved in STEP program should be avoided.
3. Preference should be given to women in recruitment of supervisors/officers under STEP program. As far as possible such employees should be absorbed by the union at the end of the STEP.
4. As far as possible NGOs should be involved in organising the WDCSs.
5. The views of the milk unions should be taken into consideration by the federation while formulating/ modifying project proposal.

Self-Help Groups

SHGs are aimed at poorest of the poor through savings and collateral free loan, the experiment has a long way to go. One need to be cautious in replication and promotion of such non-formal organisations. They have certain limitations like small savings, inadequate loan, multiplicity of organisations trying the same model, lack of institutional support, linkages, problems of interference by politicians bureaucracy, long gestation periods, etc. If some of the above lacunas are corrected and suitable measures initiated, it is hoped that micro credit would meet requirements of poorest of the poor in the country. This will also help easing government's efforts in providing reasonable livelihood to about one fourth of the Indian population.

Micro-credit movement has to be viewed from a long term perspective. Its mission goes beyond development through credit for poverty eradication. SHGs led credit delivery system has sown seeds for a self-reliant economy inculcating business culture. It also develops concern for community development and bring social and economic mobility among poor women. This framework undermines need for a deliberate policy frame in terms of technology back up, efficient marketing network, and human resource development. We need to avoid unfriendly regulations and over bureaucratization in controlling them.

General

Cooperative movement as a whole is weak, it is mostly politicized and bureaucratized. In vast majority of the cases regular elections are not conducted, wherever conducted, it is a farce. They are working as government sponsored agencies. There is a need to reform the existing cooperative law by giving powers to members and elected boards. Professionalisation of these organisations is the need of the hour. Secondly active participation of members in business activities of the societies is lacking and a number of factors (social, political, economic, religious, etc.) are responsible for this sorry state of affairs. Member education programmes are to be organised at frequent intervals with proper follow-up mechanism. Upgradation of members knowledge and skills would go a long way in improving their participation. Unions should help primaries in arranging camps and visits to successful organisations so as to bring back member loyalty which would in turn help improving health of unions. There is a need to sensitize men about the role of women in dairying and in society and benefits associated with WDCSs. Unions should diversify their product-mixes and adopt aggressive marketing strategies. Regular milk payment, bonus, price differences, etc. would bring more members into the cooperative fold. These unions should coordinate various developmental agencies (women development corporations, SC/BC/ST corporations, DRDAs, NGOs, etc.) so as to bring as many facilities as possible to members under one umbrella. This will add to convergence and weed out leakages. Unions should also focus on supply of quality technical inputs at a reasonable price round the year. In order to avoid threat from progressive private dairies, officials of the unions should be in constant touch with the members, proactive, and sensitive to their problems. A perspective plan based on holistic approach focussing attention on producer members is required for the cooperative to make them vibrant and developed in future.

Bibliography

AARO (1998), *Report of the International Workshop on Micro Entrepreneurship for Rural Women,* AARO, New Delhi.

Anonymous (1988), *The Status of Women Empowerment in All Women Dairy Cooperatives in Krishna, Chittoor, and Nalgonda Districts,* APDDCF, Hyderabad.

Anonymous (1989), *Dairy Programmes for Rural Women in Andhra Pradesh,* APDDCF, Hyderabad.

BAMUL (2000), *BAMUL: A Saga of Progress,* BAMUL, Bangalore.

Bandura, A. (1986), *Social Foundation of Thought,* Prentice-Hall, Englewood Cliffs, New Jersey.

Batra, S.L. (1996), *Employment for Women: A Study of Export Oriented Garment Industry,* Har-Anand Publications, New Delhi.

Biswas, T.K. (1999), 'Measuring women's empowerment: Some methodological issues', *Asia-Pacific Journal of Rural Development,* 9(2): 63-71.

Boserup, E. (1970), *Women's Role in Economic Development,* St. Martin's Press, New York.

Chennegowda, H. (2000), *Role of Women Dairy Co-operative Societies in White Revolution* (Mimeo), KMF, Bangalore.

Choudhury, R.C., N. Mohanan, P. Purushotham, K.P. Kumaran, A. Mohiuddin, D.P. Reddy, and D.V.R. Rao (2000), *Micro Credit Interventions in Promoting Micro Enterprises: An Exploratory Study,* NIRD, Hyderabad.

Clutterbuck, D., and C. Stuart (1992), *Makers of Management: Men and Women Who Changed the Business World,* Rupa Publishers, Calcutta.

Department of Social Welfare (1975), *Towards Equality: Report of the Committee on the Status of Women in India,* Government of India, New Delhi.

Department of Women and Child Development (1999), *Schemes for Assistance: A Handbook,* Ministry of Human Resource Development, Government of India, New Delhi.

Dubey, V.K., S.B. Singh, and J.K. Khera (1982), "Role of women in decision making with respect to animal husbandry", *Indian Journal of Home Science,* 14(2): 18-20.

ENS (2001), "Sops to Andhra Pradesh is abuse of federalism: Krishna", *Indian Express,* June 18, 2001.

Freire, P. (1970), "Education for awareness", *Risk,* 4(4):14.

Giri, V.M. (1998), *Emancipation and Empowerment of Women,* Gyan Publishing House, New Delhi.

Hapke, H.M. (1992), "An experiment in empowerment", in R. Kumar (ed.), *Women in Decision Making,* Vikas Publishing House, New Delhi.

Hashemi, S.M. (1996), "Rural credit programmes and women's empowerment in Bangladesh", *World Development,* 24(4): 635-653.

Hussain, S. (1999), "Micro finance in the selected Asian countries: An overview", *Asia-Pacific Journal of Rural Development,* 9(1): 79-97.

ILO (1995), *Gender Issues in Cooperatives: An ILO-ICA Perspective,* ILO, Geneva.

ILO (2000), *More and Better Jobs for Women and Men, The Gender Promotion Programme,* ILO, Geneva.

Jamal, S. (1989), *A Study of Role Dynamics of Farm Women in Relation to Productivity of Dairy Animals,* Ph.D. Thesis, IVRI, Izatnagar.

Jha, A.K. (2000), "Lending to the poor: Designs for credit", *Economic and Political Weekly,* 35(8 and 9): 606-609.

Jha, D. (2001), *SHGs Heralding Emergence of Genuine Cooperative Movement in India,* paper presented at the 19th Annual Convention of the Indian Society for Studies in Cooperation, held at Pune during February 2-4, 2001.

Karl, M. (1995), *Women and Employment: Participation and Decision Making,* Zed Books Limited, London.

KMF (1999), *Heribenger of Rural Prosperity:* 1974-99, KMF, Bangalore.

Kasar, D.V., D.S. Navadkar, and K.S. Birari (2001), *Cooperatives and Self-help Groups for Rural Women Empowerment and Social Upliftment,* Paper Presented at the 19th Annual Convention of the Indian Society for Studies in Cooperation, held at Pune during February 2-4, 2001.

Khan, M.A., and N. Aysha (1982), *Status of Rural Women in India,* Uppal Publishing House, New Delhi.

Kishor, R., B. Gupta, S.R. Yadav, and T.R. Singh (1999), "Role of Rural Women in Decision-making process in agriculture in district Sitapur (Uttar Pradesh)", *Indian Journal of Agricultural Economics,* 54(3): 282-286.

Kulshrestha, L.R. (2000), "Micro-finance: The New Development Paradigm for Poor Rural Women", *Kurukshetra,* 49(2): 22-31.

Kumaran, K.P. (1997), "Self-help groups: An alternative to institutional credit to the poor (A case study in Andhra Pradesh)", *Journal of Rural Development,* 16(3): 515-530.

Kumaran, K.P. (1999), "Self-help groups of the rural poor in India: An analysis", *Journal of Rural Reconstruction,* 32(2): 57-66.

Kundu, A. (2001), "Fall in sex-ratio in economically well-off states worrying", *Financial Express,* March 31, 2001.

Linton, R. (1976), *The Study of Man: An Introduction,* Appleton Press, New York.

Madhavan, E., S. Baviskar, and G. Naidu (1992), *Integrating Women into Mainstream Dairying: Report of the Evaluation Mission,* APDDCF, Hyderabad.

Menon, I.M. (1981,) *Status of Muslim Women in India: A Case Study of Kerala,* Uppal Publishing House, New Delhi.

Menon, L. (1998), *Women Empowerment and Challenge of Change,* Kanishka Publishers, New Delhi.

Moser, C. (1989), "Gender planning in the third world: Mediating practical and strategic gender needs", *World Development*, 17(11): 1799-1825.

NABARD (1989), *Studies on Self-help Groups of Rural Poor,* NABARD, Mumbai.

NABARD (1994), *Banking with the Poor: Financing Self-help Groups,* NABARD, Hyderabad.

NABARD (1995), *Study of Credit Management Groups,* NABARD, Mumbai.

NABARD (1996), *Linking Self-help Groups with Banks,* NABARD, Pune.

Neelima, K. (2001), "A commission two many", *Indian Express,* March 31, 2001.

Ojha, R.K. (2001), "Self-help groups and rural employment", *Yojana,* 45(2): 20-24.

Pandy, A.K., and Kh. B. Devi (2000), "Women in animal husbandry", *Social Welfare,* 47 (2): 6-9.

Planning Commission (1993), *Annual Plan: 1992-93,* Government of India, New Delhi.

Puhazhendhi, V., and B. Jayaraman (1999), "Increasing women's participation and employment generation among rural poor: An approach through informal groups", *Indian Journal of Agricultural Economics,* 54(3): 287-295.

Rajagopalan, S. (2001), *Women and Non-formal Cooperatives,* paper presented at the 19th Annual convention of the Indian Society for Studies in Cooperation, held at Pune during February 2-4, 2001.

Raman, N.P.Y. (2000), "Self-help groups: The Kerala experiment", *NCDC Bulletin,* 33(5 and 6): 12-14.

Ramaswamy, U., and C. Kesavan (1994), *Women Extension Programme for Dairy Development in Andhra Pradesh,* APDDCF, Hyderabad.

Rao, D.K. (1994), "Self-help groups and credit", *Artha Vijnana,* 36(3): 194-207.

Rao, N., E.M., Rogers, and A. Wayangankar (1995), Communication and Empowerment: Women Dairy Farmers of India (mimeo), University of New Mexico, Albuquerque, U.S.A.

Rao, V.M. (1995), Can Women Manage Enterprises: A Case of Piparia Cooperative Milk Society (Amul) (mimeo), VMNICM, Pune.

Rao, V.M. (1996), "Warana milk cooperatives and women producers", in Rajagopalan, R. (ed.), *Rediscovering Cooperation: Cooperation in the Emerging Context,* Anand Press, Anand.

Rao, V.M. (1997), "Time allocation of rural women: A study in Kaira district (Gujarat)" *International Journal of Development Planning and Literature,* 9 (3 and 4): 93-104.

Rao, V.M. (1998), "Kuchipudi milk society: A case study", *Social Welfare,* 45(1): 20-24.

Rao, V.M. (2000), *Developing Agro-enterprises among Farm Women: A case of AMUL,* Regency Publications, New Delhi.

Rao, V.M. (2001), *Development of Women through Dairy Cooperatives: A Study in Andhra Pradesh and Karnataka,* paper presented at the national seminar on 'Rural economy of India: Status, prospects, and policies', organised at Gokhale Institute of Politics and Economics, Pune during April 8-9, 2001.

Rogers, E.M., and A. Singhal (1993), *Communication Strategies for the Cooperative Development Programme in Indian Cooperatives,* Food and Agricultural Organisation of United Nations, Rome.

Rogers, E.M., A. Singhal, A. Wayangankar, and C.I. Shefner (1993), *Women's Empowerment through Indian Dairy Cooperatives,* paper presented at the International Communication Association, Sydney.

Rowlands, J. (1997), *Questioning Empowerment,* Oxfam, Oxford.

Sen, D., and J. Rani (1990), "Women in Dairying: A case study", *Journal of Rural Development,* 9(5): 809-831.

Sengupta, N. (1998), "Empowerment: A socio-psychological approach to self help group formation", *Prajnan,* 25(4): 533-535.

Sharma, M., and U. Vanjani (1989), "Women's work is never done: Dairy development and health in the lives of rural women in Rajasthan", *Economic and Political Weekly,* 27(17): WS38-WS44.

Singh, V.K., R. Singh, and G.K. Bama (1991), "Decision making and farm involvement of Assamese rural women", *Rural India,* 54(2): 46-48.

Srilatha, B. (1994), "The meaning of women's empowerment: New concepts from action", in Sen, G., A. Germain, and L.C. Chen (ed.), *Population Policies Reconsidered: Health, Empowerment, and Rights,* Harward School of Public Health, Boston.

Stub, H.R. (1975), *The Sociology of Education,* The Dorsey Press, Illinois.

Tapan, N. (2000), *Need for Women Empowerment,* Rawat Publications, Jaipur.

Uphoff, N. (1992), "Local institutions and participation for sustainable development", *IIED Gatekeeper Series,* No. 31, London.

Vajpayee, A.B. (2001), "Give women the freedom of choice", *Social Welfare,* 47(11): 3-4.

Verhagen, K. (1987), *Self-help Promotion: A Challenge to the NGO Community,* Royal Tropical Institute, Amsterdam.

Wayangankar, A., and S.N. Singh (1992), *Cooperative Development Programme of the NDDB,* paper present at the Institute of Rural Management, Anand.

Weinberg, C. (1971), *Education and Social Problems,* The Free Press, New York.

Appendix 1.1

Support to Training and Employment Programme for Women (STEP)

The Concept

The programme was launched in 1986 as a measure to ensure well being of women in traditional informal sectors. The project is sponsored by the Department of Women and Child Development, Ministry of Human Resources Development, Government of India. The programme aims at increasing self-reliance and autonomy of women by enhancing their productivity and enabling them to take up income generation activities. It provides training for skill upgradation to poor and assetless women in the traditional sectors like agriculture, animal husbandry and dairying, fisheries, handlooms, handicrafts, khadi and village industries, sericulture, social forestry, and wasteland development (Department of Women and Child Development, 1999).

Objectives

The project advocates integrated package of inputs aiming at overall development of women in traditional sectors. Ultimate endeavour of the project is to develop women to thrive on a self-sustaining basis in the market place with minimal governmental support and intervention after the project is completed. Specific objectives of the project are to:

(a) provide training for upgradation of skills,

(b) mobilize women in small viable groups and making facilities a variable through training and access to credit, and

(c) enable groups of women to take up employment-cum-income generation programmes of their own, and provide support services for further improving training and employment conditions of women.

Implementing Agencies

The scheme is proposed to be implemented through public sector organisation, District Rural Development Agencies, co-operatives, and voluntary organizations working in rural areas with legal status as a society registered under the Societies Registration Act of 1860 or under the corresponding state acts. Recipients of financial assistance under STEP are required to be bodies, organizations or agencies working in rural areas, although their headquarters may be located in urban areas. These organisations should have adequate infrastructure, necessary technical expertise in the sector, and financial soundness with facilities/resources for undertaking this project.

Target Group

The target group to be covered under the project includes marginalised, assetless rural women, and urban poor. This includes wage labourers, unpaid daily workers, female headed households, migrant labourers, tribals, and other dispossessed groups.

Project Implementation

The functionaries of implementing agencies and link agencies/NGOs involved would initially be given a suitable organistion towards scope, and objectives for effective implementation of the project. Sensitization towards women's issues will be an integral part of training at all levels. Women beneficiaries will be given training on group formation, skill upgradtion, management of primary producer cooperatives, entrepreneurship skills, marketing awareness about their rights, gender concern, etc. The implementing agency will help in providing of raw materials, ensure proper marketing and tie-ups for credit facilities, and marketing of the produce during the project period. It will also help women to manage their activity within the group once the project is completed.

Pattern of Assistance

In percentage terms funding pattern will be restricted in the following manner of the total project cost:

Funding Pattern under STEP

Sl. No.	*Item of expenditure*	*% to total cost*
1.	Administration and the project staff	6
2.	Training: technical skill and orientation of Beneficiaries and project functionaries	20
3.	Infrastructure including marketing support, quality control and managerial support	6
4.	Raw material for training including equipment and other material required for training	25
5.	Establishment of cooperatives, mobilizing and strengthening of field level setups where such support is not available	10
6.	Support service	8
7.	Overriding costs	6
	Total	100

Under this programme, upto 90% of the project cost is given by the Government of India and the remaining 10% will have to be borne by the implementing agency from its own sources or through sources other than Government of India. Grants are released to the implementing agencies in two instalments each year. The project should cover atleast 500 beneficiaries and the maximum could be 10000 beneficiaries.

The proposal in the prescribed format should be sent through the state government to:

The Deputy Secretary (STEP)
Department of Women & Child Development,
1st Floor, Jeevandeep Building,
Sansad Marg,
New Delhi 110 001.

Documents to be Enclosed

1. A copy of registration certificate.
2. Article of Association and constitution of the organisation.
3. List of members of the executive committee with their occupation and background.
4. Audited statement of accounts for the last 2 years.
5. A copy of the latest annual report.
6. Map of the project area.
7. State government recommendation.

Appendix 1.2

District-wise List of Selected WDCSs

State/District	*WDCSs*	*Taluka/Block*
Andhra Pradesh		
1. Ongole	1. Morlapadu	Tangutur
	2. Eluribalipuram	Chimkurti
	3. Konakanametla	Konakanametla
	4. Chapalamadugu	Yarragondapalam
	5. Naidupalam	Yarragondapalam
	6. Gangavaram	Yarragondapalam
	7. Hassanabad	Dornala
	8. Ramchandra vote	Dornala
2. Warangal	1. Kakkiralapally	Wardhannapet
	2. Kesavapur	Rayaparthy
	3. Chelvai	Rayaparthy
	4. Madepally	Govindaraopet
	5. Mariyapalam	Nellabally
	6. Kothur	Narametla
	7. Lingala Ghanapur	Rayaparthy
	8. Gunturpalli	Narmetta
3. Chittoor	1. Kamaluru	Tavanampalli
	2. Gallavallavuru	Tavanampalli
	3. Tiruvanampalli	Tavanampalli
	4. T.Kurapalli	Tavanampalli
	5. Gurralamitta	V. Kota
	6. Belu Palli	Baireddipalli
	7. K Enumulavaripalle	Madanapalle
	8. Pulavandlapalle	Madanapalle

State/District	*WDCSs*	*Taluka/Block*
Karnataka		
1. Bellary-Raichur	1. Chilagodu	Hagaribommanahalli
	2. Nellukudure	Hagaribommanahalli
	3. Ammanakari	Kudligi
	4. Gudadur	Bellary
	5. Jagannadhapuram Camp	Sindhanur
	6. Hanumannagar Camp	Sindhanur
	7. Singanala	Gangavati
	8. Ganesh Camp	Sindhanur
2. Belgaum	1. Akkatangerhal	Gokak
	2. Balobal	Gokak
	3. Sattigeri	Savadatti
	4. M.Thimmapur	Ramadurg
	5. Tondikatti	Ramadurg
	6. Hulloli	Hukkeri
	7. Chikkadinnikop	Khanapur
	8. Asoga	Khanapur
3. Belgaum	1. Kamakshipura	Bangalore North
	2. Chagalete	Bangalore North
	3. Yalachagere	Nelamangla
	4. Somalapura	Hoskote
	5. Kotamaranahalli	Chennapatna
	6. Basavanapura	Ramanagaram
	7. Thirumagonda-nahally	Anekal
	8. Railway Gollahally	Nelamangla

Index

❑❑❑